DIALECTS—U.S.A.

by
Jean Malmstrom and Annabel Ashley

Based on the chapter 'The Dialects of American English' by Raven I. McDavid, Jr., in *The Structure of American English*, by W. N. Francis, with permission of the author and the publisher.
Copyright © 1958 The Ronald Press Company.

NATIONAL COUNCIL OF TEACHERS OF ENGLISH
508 South Sixth Street, Champaign, Illinois

This publication is sponsored by the
Commission on the English Language
of the
National Council of Teachers of English

PREFACE

This book has been written in response to the need for a serious and authentic treatment of regional variety in American English suitable for use in secondary schools. In the past, our schools have neglected this aspect of our language, in spite of its unique combination of genuine practical value and perennial fascination. In an era when the increased mobility of the American people and the prevalence of a nationwide network of oral communication bring large numbers of Americans into almost daily contact with the speech of other regions beside their own, it seems hardly necessary to say that some dispassionate and objective knowledge about the variety of our speech is valuable for all. It is a rare classroom nowadays which does not show a mixture of dialects. Students are invariably fascinated by speech differences and eager to learn more about them. And since relatively little technical linguistic knowledge is required to understand and explore this subject, it is well adapted to secondary school study.

The authors are particularly well suited for their task. Mrs. Malmstrom, who is Associate Professor of English at Western Michigan University, has made it her special interest to interpret the findings of professional dialectologists to nonspecialist teachers and students of English. Mrs. Ashley, an experienced senior high school teacher, has prepared and taught materials on American dialects with signal success in the schools of Portland, Oregon. The Commission on the English Language of the National Council of Teachers of English encouraged them to write the book. The finished work more than fulfills the expectations of the Commission and receives its full endorsement.

Brown University
February 1963

W. N. Francis
Director
Commission on the English Language, NCTE

ACKNOWLEDGEMENTS

For inspiration, encouragement, and assistance, the authors are grateful to all the members of the NCTE Commission on the English Language. Special thanks are due to its director, Professor W. Nelson Francis, and to Professors Harold B. Allen, Sumner Ives, and Albert H. Marckwardt, who read the original manuscript and offered trenchant criticisms. Appreciation for valuable advice and help is also extended to Professor Raven I. McDavid, Jr., of the University of Chicago and to Dr. Norman K. Hamilton, Assistant Superintendent in Charge of Curriculum, and Miss Elsie May Cimino, Assistant Supervisor of Language Arts, Portland (Oregon) Public Schools. Sincere thanks are due also to Dean and Richard Hauck, and to Julian Freund—one present and two future teachers of English—and especially to our husbands, Vincent F. Malmstrom and Dr. Carl G. Ashley.

This book is not a work of original research since neither author is a dialect geographer. The dialect geographers of the United States form a small group of highly trained researchers who are gradually providing originally collected data for the use of scholars, textbook writers, and teachers. To a large extent the material in this book is based on two kinds of published material, both of which are listed in the following bibliography. First there are articles and books produced by the dialect geographers themselves; these are starred in the bibliography. Second there are derivative articles and books written by people who are using the original data collected by the dialect geographers; these items are unstarred in the bibliography.

In addition to these published materials, unpublished maps and field records of the Linguistic Atlas of the Upper Midwest were graciously made available by the director, Professor Harold B. Allen, between 1952 and 1958. During these same years Professors Albert H. Marckwardt, Raven I. McDavid, Jr., and Virginia G. McDavid were similarly generous with maps made from the unpublished field records of the Linguistic Atlas of the North-Central States. To these dialect geographers the authors most gratefully acknowledge fundamental indebtedness.

Jean Malmstrom
Annabel Ashley

BIBLIOGRAPHY OF SOURCES FOR DIALECTS—U.S.A.

(Starred items are publications of the dialect geographers of the Linguistic Atlas of the United States. Unstarred items are derivative publications based, wholly or partly, on the findings of the Atlas researchers.)

*Allen, Harold B. "Minor Dialect Areas of the Upper Midwest," *Publication of the American Dialect Society,* 30 (1958) 3-16.

*_____. "Semantic Confusion: A Report from Atlas Files," *Publication of the American Dialect Society,* 33 (1960) 3-13.

*_____. "The Linguistic Atlas of the Upper Midwest of the United States," *Orbis,* Tome I, No. 1 (1952) 89-94.

*Atwood, E. Bagby. *The Regional Vocabulary of Texas.* Austin: University of Texas Press, 1962.

*_____. *A Survey of Verb Forms in the Eastern United States.* Ann Arbor: University of Michigan Press, 1953.

*_____. "Words of the Southwest," *The Round Table of the South-Central College English Association,* 2 (May 1961) 1.

*Babington, Mima, and E. Bagby Atwood. "Lexical Usage in Southern Louisiana," *Publication of the American Dialect Society,* 36 (1961) 1-24.

*Bloch, Bernard. "Interviewing for the Linguistic Atlas," *American Speech,* 10 (1935) 3-9.

Bryant, Margaret M., ed. *Current American Usage.* New York: Funk and Wagnalls Company, 1962.

*Davis, Alva Lee, and Raven I. McDavid, Jr. "Shivaree: an Example of Cultural Diffusion," *American Speech,* 24 (1949) 249-255.

Drake, James A. "The Effects of Urbanization on Regional Variety," *American Speech,* 36 (1961) 17-33.

Hankey, Clyde T. "A Colorado Word Geography," *Publication of the American Dialect Society,* 34 (1960).

_____. "Semantic Features and Eastern Relics in Colorado Dialect," *American Speech,* 36 (1961) 266-270.

Ives, Sumner. "Dialect Differentiation in the Stories of Joel Chandler Harris," *American Literature,* 17 (March 1955) 88-96.

_____. "A Theory of Literary Dialect," *Tulane Studies in English,* 2 (New Orleans, 1950) 137-182.

*Kimmerle, Marjorie, Raven I. McDavid, Jr., and Virginia G. McDavid. "Problems of Linguistic Geography in the Rocky Mountain Area," *Western Humanities Review,* 5 (1951) 249-264.

*Kurath, Hans. *A Word Geography of the Eastern United States.* Ann Arbor: University of Michigan Press, 1949.

*_____, and Raven I. McDavid, Jr. *The Pronunciation of English in the Atlantic States.* Ann Arbor: University of Michigan Press, 1961.

*Kurath, Hans, *et al. Handbook of the Linguistic Geography of New England.* Washington, D. C.: American Council of Learned Societies, 1939.

Malmstrom, Jean. "A Study of the Validity of Textbook Statements about Certain Controversial Grammatical Items in the Light of Evidence from the Linguistic Atlas." Ph.D. Dissertation. University of Minnesota, 1958.

*Marckwardt, Albert H. *American English.* New York: Oxford University Press, 1959.

*_____. "Principal and Subsidiary Dialect Areas in the North-Central States," *Publication of the American Dialect Society,* 27 (1957) 3-15.

*McDavid, Raven I., Jr. "American Dialect Studies since 1939," *Philologica,* 4 (1949) 43-48.

*_____. "The Position of the Charleston Dialect," *Publication of the American Dialect Society,* 23 (1955) 35-53.

*_____. "Two Decades of the Linguistic Atlas," *Journal of English and Germanic Philology,* 50 (1951) 101-110.

*_____. "The Dialects of American English," in W. Nelson Francis, *The Structure of American English.* New York: Ronald Press, 1958.

*_____, and Virginia McDavid. *A Compilation of the Work Sheets of The Linguistic Atlas of the United States and Canada.* Ann Arbor: The Linguistic Atlas of the United States and Canada, 1951.

*_____. "Grammatical Differences in the North-Central States," *American Speech,* 35 (1960) 5-19.

*_____. "The Linguistic Atlas of New England," *Orbis,* Tome I, No. 1 (1952) 95-103.

Pyles, Thomas. *Words and Ways of American English.* New York: Random House, 1952.

*Reed, Carroll E. *American Dialects.* Seattle: University of Washington Press, 1958.

*_____. "The Pronunciation of English in the Pacific Northwest," *Language,* 37 (1961) 559-564.

*_____. "Word Geography of the Pacific Northwest," *Orbis,* Tome VI, No. 1 (1957) 86-93.

*Reed, David W. "Eastern Words in California," *Publication of the American Dialect Society,* 21 (1954) 3-15.

Thomas, Charles K. "Regional Variations in American Pronunciation," *An Introduction to the Phonetics of American English,* 2nd ed. New York: Ronald Press, 1958.

*Van Riper, William R. "Oklahoma Words," *The Round Table of the South-Central College English Association,* 2 (May 1961) 3.

*Wood, Gordon R. "An All-South Survey," *The Round Table of the South-Central College English Association,* 2 (May 1961) 3.

*_____. "Word Distribution in the Interior South," *Publication of the American Dialect Society,* 35 (1961) 1-16.

*_____. "Word Patterns of the South," *The Round Table of the South-Central College English Association,* 3 (May 1962) 1-2.

CONTENTS

CHAPTER I

DIALECT DIFFERENCES AND THEIR CAUSES

INTRODUCTION

One of the most exciting facts about overseas travel is that each time you cross a border into a new country on the continent of Europe you hear a new language spoken—French, German, Spanish, Italian, Swedish, or one of many others. Each of these languages is clearly different from the others. Each must be learned separately. A language is a set of sounds which human beings make with their vocal organs—lungs, throat, mouth—and which they organize into patterns to use as a means of carrying on the affairs of their society.

Crossing the English Channel to Great Britain, however, you might expect such differences to disappear, since English is the language of the British Isles. To your surprise, you discover that the English of the East End of London—cockney English—is quite different from the English of the Edinburgh Scotsman, and that often you yourself cannot understand either kind of English. Furthermore, you soon learn that these are only two among the many other kinds of English which are spoken in the British Isles. Each of these different kinds of English is a different dialect of English.

Thankfully, you return to the United States where, you think, everybody speaks the same kind of English. But what do you discover? An hour or two at the television set proves certainly that the Texas cowboy's speech is different from the New York cab driver's; the Alabama farmer's from the Massachusetts farmer's. There are, in other words, different dialects of American English, too, just as there are of British English. Nevertheless, after listening a minute or two to these speakers of American English, you can understand them without much trouble. You may correctly conclude, therefore, that dialectal differences in American English are less noticeable than those in British English, even though the United States is a much larger country than the British Isles and has been the "Great Melting Pot" for immigrants from many different countries of the world.

A FEW DEFINITIONS

What exactly is meant by "dialect," as the word is used here in discussing living language? Furthermore, what exactly is the difference between a "dialect" and a "language"?

We may begin by stating what a dialect is not. It is not the unusual and strange-sounding accent and word usage of a foreign-born person. Such a speaker learned English as a foreign language after he had mastered his own native tongue. His spoken English may be dramatically different from yours, but the difference is individual, belonging to him alone. His pronunciations, word choices, and sentence patterns are influenced by those of his native language.

The word "dialect," however, is associated not with individuals but with speech communities. A speech community is a group of people who are in constant communication with one another. Such a group speaks its own dialect; that is, the members of the group have certain language habits in common. For example, a family is a speech community; the members of the family talk together constantly, and certain words have certain special meanings within the family group. Or, the people who belong to your class in school form a speech community, sharing certain special ways of talking together—the latest slang, for instance. The people who work together in a single office are a speech community. Larger speech communities may be the members of a single occupation or profession. Carpenters share certain typical carpentry terms; lawyers converse using special legal terms.

An even larger speech community is the people who live in a certain geographic region. Such regional speech communities are the special concern of this book. The study of such speech communities is called "dialect geography," "linguistic geography," or "area linguistics." The scholar who studies regional varieties of a language is called "a dialect geographer," or "a linguistic geographer," or "a dialectologist."

When these scholars use the term *dialect,* it has a specific and scientific meaning, without any negative or derogatory connotations. By "dialect," linguistic geographers mean a variety of *speech* which is used in a certain locality or region and which differs in pronunciation, vocabulary, and grammar from other varieties spoken in other localities or regions. Furthermore, local or regional dialects differ from the standard language—the "book words" that could be used in any region of the country.

Sometimes, in nonscientific usage, certain other words are confused with the term *dialect.* Let's examine four of these words here: *localism, colloquialism, slang,* and *jargon.* A *localism* is a dialect form; that is, it is characteristic of a particular place or region. Contrariwise, a *colloquialism* has no connection with geography. It refers instead to a form that is characteristic of relaxed, informal conversation. Everybody uses colloquialisms because everybody converses with his friends. Colloquialisms are perfectly proper and natural in spoken English; the word has no negative or derogatory connotations. A writer, of course, avoids colloquialisms unless he is deliberately reporting oral conversation or trying to reflect it by his style of writing. *Slang* is one very popular form of extremely informal language. It is full of clipped and shortened word forms, newly invented words, old words used with new meanings, and wild, exotic figures of speech. Basically, it is violent metaphor. Usually slang is used by a rather small and intimate speech community; knowing the proper slang is a sign of belonging to the group. Among its users it becomes quickly popular and quickly dated. The French call slang *la langue verte,* "the green language," thereby recognizing its vitality. Slang sometimes enriches the standard language, though only its most useful coinages endure.

Our last term is *jargon.* Generally defined, jargon is a type of language which contains an unusually large number of words unfamiliar to the average user of the language. These words are characteristic of a particular occupation, hobby, or social group. The term *jargon* is often used disapprovingly by persons who lack knowledge of the specialized field under discussion. They feel frequently that the users of jargon are deliberately trying to be unnecessarily obscure and esoteric.

We may return now to our second big question: what exactly is the difference between a dialect and a language?

A dialect is the variety of language of a single homogeneous speech community. As long as each dialect is understandable by the speakers of its neighboring dialect, we are dealing with the same language, even though speakers who are separated by three or four intervening dialects may not be able to understand each other.

However, when the majority of members of one speech community cannot understand the speech of another speech community, then they speak different languages. Thus some languages may stretch over large geographic areas, as English does in the United States, with only relatively small differences in the different regions. On the other hand, many separate languages may exist within a relatively small geographic area, as the languages of Europe exist side by side on that continent.

In summary, we may say that a language is usually a composite structure of overlapping dialects and that each dialect within the language is a composite structure of overlapping idiolects. An idiolect is the speech pattern of one individual at one particular time of his life.

KINDS OF DIALECT DIFFERENCES

Linguistic geography reveals that dialect differences are of three kinds: differences in pronunciation, differences in vocabulary, and differences in grammar.

1. *Differences in Pronunciation*

Differences in pronunciation are of two types: systematic and individual. A systematic difference is one that affects a whole group of words in a similar way. For instance, in Eastern New England, the sound of "r" is consistently lost except before vowels. In this same geographic region, the sound of "r" often appears from nowhere between two vowel sounds, as in "the idea*r* of it." Furthermore, the same phenomena occur in New York City and in the South also. Many such systematic differences occur in American English pronunciation.

Individual differences, the second kind of pronunciation differences, affect only a single word or a group of closely related words. Probably the best known of such differences is that which affects the verb *grease* and the adjective *greasy*. Southern speakers pronounce both these words with a "z" sound, whereas Northern speakers pronounce them with an "s" sound. Another interesting group is *merry, Mary,* and *marry.* Many speakers pronounce these three words so that they all rhyme. However, in Pennsylvania *Mary* rhymes with *merry* but not with *marry.* In the South, none of the three words rhymes with either of the other two. Such individual differences in pronunciation—and there are many in the United States—are highly interesting but not really so important as the larger systematic differences.

The standard alphabet cannot record such systematic or individual differences in pronunciation. The professional linguistic geographer uses a highly detailed phonetic alphabet to make his field records. The student can easily learn and use a simpler set of symbols to record the variations he meets in his dialect studies. The symbols of the International Phonetic Alphabet (called "IPA") are usually listed in dictionaries and serve well to help students transcribe speech. Phonetic transcription emphasizes again the large differences between speaking and writing. Remember that the study of dialect is the study of speech, not writing. The indication of dialect in literature by means of distorted spellings presents difficult problems for an author. These literary problems will be discussed in Chapter VI.

2. *Differences in Vocabulary*

The second kind of contrast concerns differences in vocabulary. These differences are the easiest to observe and probably the most interesting to discuss. Notice these groups of words; they all refer to the same thing but are the different names which are used in different regions of the United States.

creek, stream, brook, run, branch, fork, prong, gulf, binnekill, binacle, rivulet, riverlet, gutter, kill, bayou, burn

cottage cheese, clabber cheese, pot cheese, Dutch cheese, smear cheese, smear case, sour-milk cheese, curd, home-made cheese

seesaw, teetering board, teeter-totter, dandle, tilt, tilts, ridy-horse, hicky-horse, teeter-horse, see-horse, tiltamo

peanuts, ground peas, goobers, grubies, pinders, ground nuts, grounuts, ground almonds

If you have listened to speakers in different parts of the United States with careful attention, you probably can think of other similar sets of words.

3. *Differences in Grammar*

The third kind of contrast involves differences in grammar. For instance, a majority of Northern speakers prefer *dove* as the past tense of *dive;* a majority of Southern speakers prefer *dived.* In Midland areas, both forms occur, with *dove* preferred by the more modern and better educated speakers. Another grammatical example is the use of *all the farther* in a sentence like, "Two miles is all the farther he can go." People in New England use *as far as,* not *all the farther,* although it is often used in other regions on the Atlantic Seaboard and in the North-Central States of Wisconsin, Michigan, Illinois, Indiana, Kentucky, and Ohio. Farther west, it is heard in Minnesota and Iowa but not in Nebraska or North and South Dakota.

REASONS FOR DIALECT DIFFERENCES

If some mighty dictator conquered the world and ordered all the world's people to speak one uniform language, and if this dictator miraculously enforced his decree, nevertheless within one generation this language would change. Each child, no matter how hard he tries to copy his parents' language, always speaks slightly differently from the way they do. These changes pile up through the years so that eventually we have forms of the language as different as Shakespeare's is from yours. Furthermore, language changes differently in different parts of the world.

The development of the Romance languages—especially Italian, French, Spanish, and Rumanian—from Latin is a fine example of a change in which a single parent language evolved through the centuries into several daughter languages. The Roman soldiers and administrators who conquered, occupied, and governed the provinces of the Roman empire did not speak the formal, precise Latin which you study in school. They spoke a more fluid and flexible form of the language. It was called "Latin of the People" or "Vulgar Latin." (The Latin word, *vulgus,* means "the crowd.") Thus even in the mouths of these Romans the Latin of literature and the Latin of speech were different. Further changes accumulated until finally various Romance languages developed. These languages are called "Romance" because they came from the Roman language.

The forces which cause such dialectal differences are strong and interesting. These forces are apparent in all parts of the world, but we shall focus on the United States.

1. *Early Settlement History*

Any large or important group which settles in any particular region will contribute some elements of its language to the speech of its new home. Looking back to the history of the thirteen original colonies from which our country grew, we see first a large migration of English people. They came chiefly from the southern and midland counties of England, but there were some families from Yorkshire, Lancashire, and even the farther north counties of England. Each of these counties in England had its own local dialect, and the settlers brought these dialects to the New World with them. Gradually, in the course of several generations, these dialects were blended into distinctively American dialects. Later, Ulster Scotsmen, Palatinate Germans, Dutchmen, all added important words to American English. These contributions characterized the English of the locality where each of these different population groups settled. The Spanish in California also made their distinctive contribution to American English, as did the French in Louisiana.

2. *Population Migrations*

Other dialect differences are created by the movements of people from one region of the country to another. Citizens of the United States have always been highly mobile. The Westward Movement carried speech forms from Pennsylvania west to Ohio, and from New York to Michigan. Migrations north up the Mississippi River to southeastern Minnesota spread Midland words into that Northern dialect area. A small area in southeastern Nebraska has certain Northern speech forms apparently brought there after the Civil War by a number of New York and Ohio families who migrated west into the east Platte River Valley.

3. *Physical Geography*

Mountain ranges, rivers, marshes, and deserts may affect the character of different dialects. In some cases, such natural phenomena may block the spread of certain words or expressions. In other cases, they may add words to the vocabulary to name geographic features peculiar to certain regions. For instance, in Colorado the word *park* is used to mean mountain meadow in the mountainous area and in the nearby foothill communities but not elsewhere in the state. In Colorado *prairie dog owl* is heard only in communities on or near the eastern plains of the state. In that part of Colorado, the expression "The wind is rising" or "The wind is raising" seems very appropriate. In this arid locality, you can actually "see" the wind from a distance.

4. *Cultural Centers*

Great cities—like New York, Philadelphia, Charleston, Chicago, St. Louis, San Francisco—acquire prestige and become influential socially, economically, and culturally. They dominate the regions around them, and their speechways are copied by speakers in these surrounding regions. The influence of the great cities on the Atlantic Seaboard is second only to that of the original settlement history in determining dialects there. For instance, words have spread westward from Philadelphia to the Alleghenies and southward along Delaware and Chesapeake Bay. Some of these typical words are *pavement* for 'side walk,' *baby coach* for 'baby carriage,' *flannel cakes* for 'griddle cakes,' *button wood* for 'sycamore,' *coal oil* for 'kerosene,' and *snake doctor* for 'dragon fly.'

5. *Social Structure of the Area*

In any country where social classes are clearly defined, the dialects of each class will show unmistakable differences. In England, for instance, the speech of the Wessex peasants in Hardy's novels is strikingly distinct from the speech of his upper-class characters. The latter speak Received Standard English. In the United States, no such sharp dialectal lines divide social classes. All children here are taught standard English in our schools. This is the language used to transact the important affairs of our country. As you might expect, a person's dialect tends to reflect the length of time he has spent in school. The college graduate speaks differently from the high school graduate; both of them speak differently from the person who has had an eighth grade education or less. In this book, we are not chiefly concerned with these socioeducational differences. We are studying the regional differences which are observable in the standard English of cultivated speakers.

6. *Late Immigrations*

The dialects of a region may reflect the arrival of a large group of new immigrants with a native language different from that of the inhabitants of the region to which they migrate. If members of this new group introduce new articles or ideas, their names for these innovations may be added to the old language. For example, about the middle of the nineteenth century, crowds of newcomers arrived in the United States from Germany. Consequently, English was soon enriched with many new words—*delicatessen, pretzel, zwieback, frankfurter,* and especially *hamburger*—to name only a few.

SUMMARY

In this first chapter we have looked at the field of linguistic geography in broad general fashion, defining a few essential terms, noting the three kinds of dialect differences, and examining the most important reasons for such differences. In the next chapter we will consider linguistic geography in the United States in greater detail.

SUGGESTIONS FOR STUDY

Keep a Language Notebook

A language notebook provides a means of recording and studying your course in linguistic geography. In it you may file new words and organize notes taken from your text, lectures, discussions, and supplementary reading. These notes will form the basis for your preparation for tests as well as for oral and written reports. You will find ideas for materials to file in your notebook listed first under the *Suggestions for Study* for each of the following chapters of the text.

Test Your Comprehension

1. Name the three major kinds of dialect differences. Add to each an example not supplied by the text.

2. Explain the meaning of the terms *localism, colloquialism, slang,* and *jargon,* and give an example of each.

3. Explain the meaning of the terms *systematic differences* and *individual differences* in pronunciation. Give examples of both.

4. What distinction should you make between the variations in the speech of people living in different areas of this country and those characteristic of persons born in another country who learned English as a second language?

5. List reasons for dialect differences. Illustrate each.

Add to Your Vocabulary

Find in the text a definition of each of the following terms: *language, dialect,* and *speech community.* Copy each word in its context into your language notebook. Under each quotation write a sentence of your own using the word in such a way that its meaning is clearly indicated.

Describe Sound by Using Symbols

When you study differences in the pronunciation of the same word in different dialects, you will find it necessary to describe sounds. Learning a set of symbols from a standard phonetic or phonemic system enables you to describe to others the pronunciation of a word. When you have learned the system that your teacher recommends, practice transcribing several passages in symbols. You will soon discover that you must record words as they sound, ignoring, for the moment, their spelling.

Class use of pronunciation symbols

1. Transcribe the first two sentences of the *Introduction* in Chapter I.

2. Two or three students volunteer to write their transcriptions on the blackboard. Each then translates his passage into speech. Do you agree with his use of symbols? If not, does your point of disagreement concern the use of consonants or vowels? Does the difference between his transcription and yours lie in the choice of symbols or in actual difference in pronunciation? What does this indicate concerning the existence of individual differences in the speech of people in the same group? What is the term used to describe these differences?

Individual use of pronunciation symbols

1. In your written reports, use symbols to represent dialectal differences in pronunciation.

2. Use symbols to indicate pronunciation in recording vocabulary words.

3. Use symbols in recording sounds in your foreign language study.

Consider Your Class as a Speech Community

Although the members of your class probably speak the same kind of English, you may be able to detect some individual differences in pronunciation and vocabulary. Write on the blackboard, one at a time, the following words: *grease, greasy, merry, Mary,* and *marry.* Each student pronounces the word as he normally would while the others in the class listen. Repeat this process with each word, recording any variation in pronunciation on the board by means of pronunciation symbols if you have learned the IPA or the Trager-Smith phonemic system.

Having detected differences, can you account for them by determining the regional background of the student? By selecting a list of items from the examples given of differences in vocabulary and grammar in Chapter I, you can find and account for variations of these kinds in the speech of people in the class.

Write a Theme

Describe your family as a speech community, recording differences in speech and finding reasons for these in the regional background, profession, occupation, or interests of members of your family. Notice differences in pronunciations of words, choice of words, and choice of grammatical forms. These differences will highlight the fact that each member of your family speaks his own idiolect, even though he belongs to the family speech community. Titles like "Potpourri" and "The Language of the Clan" suggest interesting discussions.[1]

Select for discussion the vocabulary characteristic of a particular speech community such as a profession, occupation, hobby, interest, or sport. Titles might range from "Legal Language" through "Rockhound Dialect" and "Words That Make Music" to "Slalom!"

Compare American English to British English. Limit your comment to one set of terms: for example, the language of road signs in America as compared to that commonly used in England.

Analyze and discuss the origin and place of slang in the language of high school people. Select terms that are in good taste, original, apt, and amusing.

---

[1] *Guide for High School English* (Portland, Oregon, 1962), p. 304, by permission of the Portland Public Schools.

CHAPTER II

LINGUISTIC GEOGRAPHY IN THE U. S. A.

INTRODUCTION

When you coast down a hill lying face down on a wagon or sled, do you go *belly-bunt, belly-bust, belly-bumps, belly-gut, belly-flop, bellity-bump, belly-kuhchunk, belly-booster, belly-wop, belly-whack, belly-whomp, belly-slide, belly-slam,* or do you go downhill *boy fashion, scooting,* or *head fo'most*—or do you have some other words to describe what you are doing? All of the expressions listed above are used in different parts of the United States to name this favorite sport of young people. These are the kinds of different expressions—technically called "variants" —which interest the linguistic geographer. Probably everyone in our country is an amateur linguistic geographer in this sense. All of us are fascinated by comparing our way of saying something with other ways which we may meet in our travels or on television, or by talking with persons from other parts of the country. We laugh together because other people call our doughnuts *crullers, fried-cakes, fat-cakes, riz doughnuts, olicooks, rings,* or *fossnocks.*

However, unlike us, the linguistic geographer is systematic in his comparisons, carefully recording and analyzing what he hears in order to plot regional and local variants in speech. His methods are exact and specific. By using them he produces what is known as a linguistic atlas. This is a set of maps or tables reporting the dialect of particular regions.

Linguistic atlases have been made for many different countries throughout the world, but we are interested here in the Linguistic Atlas of the United States. We can discuss it in detail after we 1) learn the methods by which American linguistic geographers collect, analyze, and report American English; and 2) add a few technical terms to our vocabulary.

THE SYSTEMATIC METHODS OF LINGUISTIC GEOGRAPHY

When the speech of any particular region is analyzed, the region's economic and cultural history and its geography must first be studied. In the light of this study, a set of communities within the region is selected for thorough investigation. These communities are ones which

11

have played an important part in the history of the region. Perhaps they were early permanent settlements or were located on vital trade or migration routes. Or perhaps they were, or are, urban centers of culture and industry. Contrariwise, they might have been relatively isolated communities and therefore may have preserved older forms of the local language. Or perhaps they have a large foreign population and thus show the effects of foreign language borrowings. At any rate, these representative communities are carefully chosen to form a network which will give an adequate cross section of the region's known historical, cultural, economic, and geographic composition.

Next, individuals within each community are selected to furnish the needed information about the speech of the region. These individuals are chosen because they will fully represent the population of the community. They must range from old to young, from high to low on the social and economic scale, and from college to less than eighth grade education. In the records of the Linguistic Atlas of the United States, these informants are classified as follows:

   I.   Old-fashioned, rustic speakers of eighth grade education.
  II.   Younger, more modern speakers of high school education.
 III.   Cultured speakers of college education.

These persons, technically called "informants," are then interviewed by a trained interviewer called a "field worker," who uses a questionnaire designed to bring out words and phrases which will give regional information on pronunciation, vocabulary, and grammar. The items on the questionnaire are chosen for three main reasons: 1) because they refer to common things which will be known to most of the people of the region, 2) because they are easy to introduce into a friendly conversation, and 3) because they are known to have regional or social variants. Such items usually concern ordinary everyday life within the intimate circle of the family and the community. For example, groups of items cluster around the weather, the home, food, clothing, and the farm with its animals, crops, vehicles, and utensils. Interspersed among such vocabulary groups are others more directly concerned with grammar—on verb forms and verb phrases, on pronouns, adverbs, and prepositions.

The interview may last anywhere from six to twenty hours and is carried on in as conversational a way as possible. Using a special phonetic alphabet which can record more than four hundred differences in vowel sounds alone, the field worker writes down what the informant says about each item and how he pronounces it. The items are listed on sheets of paper called "work sheets," which are bound into notebooks. Some field workers have used tape and disc recorders to record their interviews.

Since interviewing of this sort is very expensive and time-consuming, some of the American linguistic geographers have used another method to collect dialect information. This method is the postal check list. In this method a questionnaire is sent out by mail to be filled in and returned by an informant. In this way a much larger sampling of speakers can be made, even though their responses usually are less full and detailed than those gathered by the interview method. Differences in pronunciation are difficult to discover by this method. However, comparisons show that the check list responses substantially corroborate the findings of the field workers.

These then are the methods used in the United States for collecting information on dialects. Now we shall learn a few technical terms.

DEFINITIONS OF A FEW TECHNICAL TERMS

1. *Isogloss, Bundle of Isoglosses, Dialect Boundary, Dialect Area*

When a linguistic geographer finds an expression which is used in a certain definite region, he can often draw a line on a map of this region to show the outside edge of the area in which it occurs. This line on the map is called an isogloss, a geographic boundary showing the area in which this expression is used. He can draw other isoglosses on his map to show where other regional expressions are found too. When he has drawn quite a number of these isoglosses, he often discovers that several isoglosses match up along at least part of their length. In such cases, he has what is called a bundle of isoglosses. This bundle of isoglosses is said to be a dialect boundary, separating one dialect area from another. Isoglosses can be drawn for all three different kinds of dialect contrasts: differences in pronunciation, differences in vocabulary, and differences in grammar. Sometimes, when all the kinds of isoglosses are drawn, the linguistic geographer finds that several kinds coincide and that therefore the dialect areas can be firmly defined. More often, however, the isoglosses may space out in various ways, showing differing degrees of influence from surrounding areas.

2. *Focal Area, Relic Area, Transition Area*

The isogloss groupings, as well as the number of isoglosses, give the linguistic geographer information. If the isoglosses are closely bunched together near a large city which is a center of industry and culture, and if the dialect forms seem to be spreading out from this central core, then we have what is called a focal dialect area. On the other hand, if the isoglosses do not bunch together or center around any important city, but instead show local speech forms receding inward and actually being lost, the area is said to be a relic area. Furthermore, if the area has no sharply defined expressions of its own but seems to share forms taken from several nearby areas, it is said to be a transition area.

With these technical terms in mind, we can discuss the systematic methods by which American linguistic geographers are producing the Linguistic Atlas of the United States.

THE LINGUISTIC ATLAS OF THE UNITED STATES

Linguistic geography was well established in Europe when the proposal was made in 1929 for a linguistic atlas of the United States. This proposal was developed by carefully planned steps, with Professor Hans Kurath as director. The expense of the proposed atlas was estimated at $664,000. Because of this large estimate, it was decided to run an experimental investigation on one restricted geographic area to demonstrate the methods which would be used and to be sure that the financial estimate was correct.

The Linguistic Atlas of New England

Therefore, plans were made for a linguistic atlas of New England to include Connecticut, Rhode Island, Massachusetts, Vermont, New Hampshire, and Maine. The history of this region was thoroughly studied, and field workers were trained. Field interviewing began in 1931 and was completed twenty-five months later in September, 1933.

After this, all the field records had to be edited, analyzed, and recorded on dialect maps. Between 1939 and 1943, at a cost of about $250,000, the six large volumes of 734 maps which make up the *Linguistic Atlas of New England* were published. If you ever visit a large university library, ask a librarian to let you see these important books. The set is one of the great monuments of United States scholarship.

Three types of maps are found in the *Linguistic Atlas of New England*. The first type of map is that which shows differences in pronunciation. For instance, in most of New England the sound of "h" is present before the sound of "w" in accented syllables at the beginning of words such as *wheelbarrow, whip, whinny,* and *whicker.* However, this "h" sound is lost either wholly or partly in a narrow coastal strip of New England extending from Boston to the Kennebec River in Maine.

The second type of map is that which shows the different words New Englanders use to indicate the same object or action. For instance, the map for coasting face down shows *belly-bump, belly-bumpers,* and *belly-bumping* in coastal New England; *belly-bunt* in the upper Connecticut Valley, in Worcester County, Massachusetts, and in parts of Maine; *belly-gut* and *belly-gutter* in the lower Connecticut Valley; *belly-flop* and *belly-flopper* in Western New England; and *belly-kuhchunk* around New London, Connecticut.

The third type of map is that which shows differences in grammar. For instance, the map for the preposition in the sentence, "He isn't at home," shows that throughout New England all informants use *at* except the oldest and least educated. These informants say, "He isn't to home."

The Linguistic Atlases of the Middle Atlantic and South Atlantic States

While the editing and publication of the *Linguistic Atlas of New England* was proceeding, field work was completed for the Atlantic Seaboard states of New Jersey, New York, Pennsylvania, West Virginia, Virginia, Delaware, Maryland, North and South Carolina, and eastern Georgia. Originally, separate atlases were planned for the northern four and the southern six states, but today the two groups are combined into one large project. Again, Professor Hans Kurath was the director. The field work was done principally by two investigators: Guy S. Lowman, Jr., from 1933 till his death in 1941, and Raven I. McDavid, Jr., from 1941 to 1949, with an interlude for World War II. The field records of the Middle Atlantic and South Atlantic States still await editing and publication, which are delayed by lack of financial support.

The Linguistic Atlas of the North-Central States

In 1938, under the direction of Professor Albert H. Marckwardt, an experimental survey was begun in the states of Wisconsin, Michigan, Illinois, Indiana, Kentucky, and Ohio for the Linguistic Atlas of the North-Central States. Previous to the atlas survey, it was supposed that the American English spoken in this area was so uniform that it could be called simply "General American." This idea has now been proved false because regional differences exist in this area as they do in all other parts of the United States.

World War II interrupted work here also, but the records are now complete. There are two sets of records: one at the University of Michigan (where the Atlantic Seaboard records also are located) and the other at the University of Chicago.

The Linguistic Atlas of the Upper Midwest

The Linguistic Atlas of the Upper Midwest, the fourth regional Atlas project, began in 1947 under the direction of Professor Harold B. Allen.

It included Minnesota, Iowa, North and South Dakota, and Nebraska. More than half of the field work was done by Allen himself, and the records are now complete and are being edited for publication. These records are located at the University of Minnesota. The Linguistic Atlas of the Upper Midwest was the first regional atlas officially to adopt postal check lists to supplement field records, although they had been used unofficially in the North-Central States.

The Linguistic Atlas of the Rocky Mountain States

In 1950, work began on the Linguistic Atlas of the Rocky Mountain States, under the direction of Professor Marjorie Kimmerle. The area encompasses the states of Montana, Wyoming, Utah, Colorado, Arizona, and New Mexico. Here distances are great, population is relatively sparse, and financial support is uncertain. Even though postal check lists have been used to good advantage, only Colorado and Utah are completely investigated to date. Because the territory is so large and the financial support so uncertain, it seems best to publish the work as a series of state projects with a general loose organization rather than as a complete atlas of the total region.

The Linguistic Atlases of the Pacific Coast

The Atlas investigations on the Pacific Coast are divided into a northern part, the Pacific Northwest—including Washington, Oregon, and Idaho—under the direction of Professor Carroll E. Reed, and a southern part, consisting of California and Nevada, directed by Professor David W. Reed. In both Pacific Coast projects, postal check lists have been used to supplement field interviews. These interviews are complete in Washington, close to complete in Idaho, and under way in Oregon. The California field work is complete, and the records are being edited.

The Linguistic Atlas of Texas

The Atlas work in Texas, under the direction of Professor E. Bagby Atwood, has followed a somewhat different course from that of the other Atlas projects. The vocabulary items have been separated from the pronunciation items, and Atwood has described the vocabulary in *The Regional Vocabulary of Texas*. He intends eventually to handle the pronunciation items too, but his plans for this survey are not yet firm.

The Linguistic Atlas of the Inland South

Work in the states of Alabama, Arkansas, Florida, Louisiana, Oklahoma, Mississippi, and west Georgia has not been organized under a single director. These states are grouped here under the name "Inland South." During the past twenty-five years, Professor C. M. Wise directed

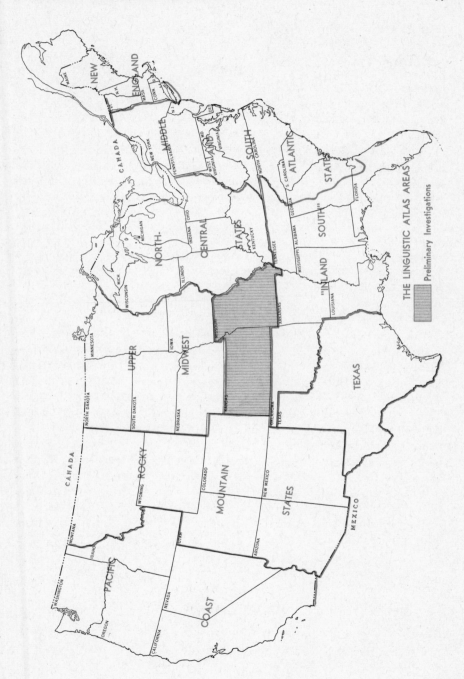

his graduate students at Louisiana State University in completing about 125 field records for different parts of Louisiana. The other states in this area have been investigated by a postal check list survey conducted by Professor Gordon Wood. He has sent out about three thousand questionnaires, selected the best thousand, and keyed them for handling by IBM procedures. He also has some tape recordings of Alabama and eastern Tennessee ready for analysis. Financial support, however, again is lacking.

In Oklahoma, Professor William R. Van Riper is director of the Oklahoma Linguistic Atlas, financed by the Oklahoma State University Research Foundation. This foundation has limited the work to Oklahoma. Each of Van Riper's fifty interviews consists of 925 items.

SUMMARY

These then are the various regional projects completed or now in progress which will make up the Linguistic Atlas of the United States. In all the work for the different projects, carefully formulated procedures have been used to collect linguistic information which will define the dialect areas of the United States of America.

The following word lists are selected from the records of the Linguistic Atlas projects. The lists include *local* as well as *regional* variants. That is, some of the terms listed are characteristic of relatively small (and often isolated) localities; others are current throughout a relatively large region. Word lists like these are not and cannot be complete. They cannot represent the infinite and unpredictable variety of variants which may be used by speakers of American English. No matter how many records a field worker makes, he must always be alert for new variants. This variety is part of the fascination of dialect study. Furthermore, the dialect areas of the Atlantic Coast—Northern, Midland, and Southern—are insufficient for classifying some of the variants found in the word lists. Many of the variants are western words, describing western customs and natural phenomena. Such words simply do not exist on the Atlantic Coast.

WORD LISTS
NOUNS
Food and Drink

APPLE COBBLER 'baked in a deep dish' apple dowdy, pan dowdy, apple slump, deep-dish apple pie, pot pie, bird's nest, family pie, deep apple pie, apple grunt, apple Jonathan

BREAD 'wheat bread, baked in loaves' white bread, light bread, bread, pan bread
'other kinds of bread made with flour' rim, wasp nest bread, riz bread, yeast bread, biscuits, hot rolls, bannocks, poverty cakes, buns, tortillas, Indian bread, potato bread, limpa, salt-rising bread
'cornbread, baked in large cakes' Johnny cake, corn pone, pone
'other kinds of bread and cakes made of corn meal' bread, spoon bread, awendaw, batter bread, egg bread, ash bread, ashcake, ash pone, hoe cake, flapjack, corn dodger, johnny cake, corn duffy, grilled bread, cracklin' bread, fatty bread, hush puppies, red-horse bread, corn sticks, muffins, corn cakes
CORN 'served on the cob' sweet corn, sugar corn, mutton corn, green-corn, roasting ears, table corn
COTTAGE CHEESE pot cheese, Dutch cheese, smear case, smear cheese, clabber cheese, sour-milk cheese, home-made cheese
DOUGHNUTS crullers, fried-cakes, fat-cakes, raised doughnuts, oli-cooks, riz doughnuts, nut cakes, rings, fossnocks
GRIDDLE CAKES pancakes, batter cakes, hot-cakes, flannel cakes, flapjacks, slapjacks, fritters, flitters
PEACHES 'cling-stone peach' plum peach, press peach, stick-stone, cleave-stone, hard peach
'free-stone peach' clear-seed peach, soft peach, clear-stone, free-seed
'stone of a peach' seed, kernel, curl, pit
PEANUTS ground peas, goobers, grubies, pinders, ground nuts, grounuts, ground almonds
SODA WATER pop, soda, tonic, soda pop
SPRING ONIONS young-onions, green-onions, shallots, scallions, rare-ripes, chibboles, toppy onions, toppies
STRING BEANS sallit beans, green beans, snap beans, snaps, wax beans, beans

Man's Other Artifacts

ANDIRONS dog irons, fire irons, handirons, fire dogs, dogs
BABY CARRIAGE baby buggy, baby cab, baby coach, buggy wagon
BED-SPREAD coverlet, coverlid, counterpane
BLACKTOP 'bituminous road' tarvia road, tarvy road, tarvy, oiled road, pavement, pave
BOULEVARD 'grass strip between sidewalk and street' grass strip, berm, parkway, parking, parking strip, tree lawn
CEMENT ROAD concrete road, hard-road, pave, pavement

CHEST OF DRAWERS   dresser, bureau, chiffonier, chifferobe

CHIMNEY   flue, smokestack, funnel

CLOTHES CLOSET   closet, press, clothes press, wardrobe, armoire

CORRAL   barnyard, barn lot, feed lot, park, back yard, stockade, night yard

COUNTY SEAT   county capital, shire town, county site, county town, parish seat

EAVES TROUGHS   gutters, spouting, canals, canales, spouts, water troughs

FAUCET   tap, spigot, spicket, hydrant, cock

FRYING PAN   skillet, spider, creeper, fry pan

GARRET   attic, sky parlor, cock loft

IRRIGATION DITCH   canal, water ditch, acequia, sakey ditch

JUNK 'old worthless furniture and implements'   clutch, rubbish, trash, plunder, trumpery

KINDLING WOOD   fat pine, pitch pine, rich pine, lightwood, lightern, pine, kindling

KITCHEN   porch, cook house, cook room, stove room, kitchen house, summer kitchen, cellar kitchen

LARIAT 'rope with loop'   lasso, reata, roping rope, rawhide rope

MANTLE SHELF   mantle piece, mantle, tussock, clock shelf, fire board, mantle board, mantle tree

OVERALLS   denims, jeans, blue jeans, blue bucks, levis, overhauls

PAPER BAG   sack, poke, toot, tote bag
  'sack made of cloth'   bag, poke, meal sack
  'burlap bag'   sack, gunny sack, crocus sack, tow sack, guano sack, coffee sack

PORCH   gallery, veranda, piazza, balcony, stoop, breezeway, dog trot, dog run

PUBLIC SQUARE   common, green, park, place, plaza, town square

ROOT CELLAR   root house, potato pit, potato cellar, potato cave, potato dugout

QUILT   comforter, comfort, comfortable, puff, soogan

SEESAW   teetering board, teeter-totter, dandle, tilt, tilts, ridy-horse, hicky-horse, cock-horse, teeter-horse, see-horse, tiltamo

SHED   ell, hillhouse, lean-to, woodhouse, woodshed, cob house, tool house, tool shed

SHIVAREE 'noisy, burlesque serenade after a wedding'   serenade, belling, dish-panning, skimmelton, callathump, reception, horning, bull-banding, drumming, salute

SITTING ROOM 'where guests are entertained' big house, parlor, front room, living room, bestroom, hall, keeping room

SOFA lounge, couch, chesterfield, davenport

STONE BOAT 'for transporting stones from field; no wheels' drag, mud boat, stone gear, stone slip, go-devil, go-dig, travois, try-boy, draw-boy

WINDOW SHADES 'roller shades' blinds, curtains, roller shades

WEATHERBOARDS clapboards, siding, weather boarding

WHARF 'where boats stop and upon which freight is unloaded' landing, pier, dock

Phenomena of Nature

BADLANDS 'unfit for cultivation' malpais, alkali flats, poverty flats, waste land, filth land, barrens

BOTTOM LAND 'flat, low-lying land along a stream, flooded in spring, plowed later' low-land, intervale, flat, flats, bottom, bottoms

COULEE 'small depression with usually dry water course' draw, seep, swale, arroyo, wash

DRAGONFLY snake doctor, snake feeder, darning needle, mosquito hawk, spindle, sewing needle, snake guarder

CREEK 'small, fresh-water stream' stream, brook, run, branch, fork, prong, gulf, binnekill, binacle, rivulet, riverlet, gutter, kill, bayou, coulee, burn

EARTHWORM angleworm, bait, mud worm, red worm, fish worm, fishing worm, ground worm, rain worm
'large earthworm' night crawler, night walker, town worm, wiggler, john jumper

HILL knob, knoll, butte, taunch

MEADOW 'low-lying grass land' swale, bayou, bayouland, mash land, prairie, dago, plains, flats, llano

MINNOWS 'a bait' minnies, shiners, minnow fish, killies, killiefish, silvers

PRAYING MANTIS walking stick, darning needle, devil's horse

RAIN 'heavy, of short duration' cloudburst, down-pour, squall, goose drownder, down-fall, gully-washer, trash-mover, down-spout, toad-strangler, lightwood knot-floater

RELATIVES people, folks, kinfolks, folkses, home folks, kinnery, relations

REMUDA 'band or herd of saddle horses' string, cavvy, caballada, caviard

SOIL dirt, earth, ground

SPIDERWEB   spider's web, cobweb, spider nest, dew web
SYCAMORE   button wood, button ball, plane tree

VERBS

The parts of phrases set off by parentheses are given to establish the context in which the item is used.

(he) CAUGHT (a cold)   caught cold, took cold, taken cold, take cold, ketched cold

(she) CLEANS UP (every morning)   tidies up, reds up, rids up

(I'm going to) COOK (some coffee)   boil, draw, steep, make

ESCORT 'to a social event'   take, carry, drag, accompany

(I'm going to) GET (supper)   make, fix

(we) INTEND (to go soon)   mean, are projectin', are letting on going, aim, are fixing, are studying on

(school) LETS OUT (at four o'clock)   turns out, is over, gets out, leaves out, closes

(she has to) LOOK AFTER (the baby)   mind, tend, take care of, see after

(you better) PITCH IN   link in, turn to, hop to, hump to it, hump yourself, lend a hand, give a hand

(she has) REARED (three children)   raised, brought up, fetched up, fotch up

(the boy) RESEMBLES (his father)   takes after, favors, features, looks like, is the spitten image of, is natured like

SIT DOWN 'invitation to sit down at table'   draw up, set up

(he) SKIPPED CLASS   played hookey, bolted, hooked Jack, played truant, laid out, bagged school, skipped school

(I) THINK (I'll have time)   guess, suppose, reckon, allow, calculate, figure

(he is) WASTING TIME   loafing on the job, soldiering, piddling, puttering around, dawdling, filling time, killing time, drawing pay

(you're going to get a) WHIPPING 'to a child'   licking, smacking, skutching, skelping, trouncing, correcting, brawsing, linting, larruping, tanning, blistering, thrashing, frailing, skinning, shellacking, switching, beating

ADJECTIVES

(he was) ALL EXCITED 'with expectation'   all of a biver, all of a trouble, all a trouble, all aflutter

(don't be so) OBSTINATE   stubborn, set, sot, pig-headed, ornery, contrary, cracky, jumptious, bull-headed, mule-headed, hard-headed

PEAKED 'as a result of ill health' skinny, shrawny, thaveless, poor, sickly, pimpin', pindlin', puny, crawny-bone, strawny-bone

(he is quite) SKILLFUL (at plowing, carpentering, odd jobs) a hand at, clever, handy, knacky, sleighty, a soon man

(she's too) SLOVENLY (for me) dutchy, tacky, sloppy, mussy, slouchy, dowdy, slack and nasty, gommy, messy

TIRED exhausted, fagged out, perished, beat out, tuckered out, tuckered, used up, done up, done in, petered out, kilt, give out, whipped, pooped, all in, bushed, blowed

TOUCHY 'easily offended' ficety, testy, touchous, fretful, short-patient

ADVERBS

(it's) ALMOST (midnight) nigh, well-nigh, nigh onto, near, nearly, pretty near

(it got) AWFULLY (cold) terribly, right, monstrous, fearfully, powerful, right smart

(it goes) CLEAR (across) clean, plum, slam, jam

KITTY-CORNERED 'of walking across an intersection or lot' cattercornered, catty-wampus, zig-zag, caper-cornered, bias-ways

(it's) RATHER (cold) kind of, sort of, middling

(he's) SOMEWHAT (better) some, a little, a mite, doing all right

PREPOSITIONS

(he is sick) AT (his stomach) to, in, on, of

(we named the child) FOR (him) at, after, from

(quarter) OF (eleven) to, till

(she's) AT (the house) to, in

(I was) UP IN (Boston) up to, over at, over to, down to, over in

SUGGESTIONS FOR STUDY

Outline the Linguistic Atlas Projects

Prepare an outline of the Linguistic Atlas projects, listing each project by name and indicating the states involved in it. Indicate the progress made in each area.

Test Your Comprehension

1. What factors govern the selection of a community for linguistic investigation? The selection of informants? In both instances, why are these particular factors important?

2. Name and describe two methods used to collect dialect information.

3. What three kinds of maps are found in the *Linguistic Atlas of New England?*

Add to Your Vocabulary

Consult a dictionary that furnishes the etymology of words for information concerning the history of the following terms: *linguistic, variant,* and *isogloss.* Write a brief statement explaining the meaning of each word in terms of the one from which it developed.

Make a Dialect Survey of Your Area

Using information supplied in Chapter IV of the text and the word lists, compile a check list of ten to twenty items designed to elicit information concerning vocabulary and grammar usage from those contacted. For each item in the list, include several choices drawn from dialectal usage in various parts of the country. At the beginning or end provide space for information pertinent to the regional background of the informant: whether he is a native of the area or not; if not, the place where he formerly lived and how long. The place of birth of parents and grandparents of the informant might be included. His education, too, should be noted. After the class has chosen the best from several sample check lists, these may be duplicated for students to use in getting information about dialect background from family and neighbors.

As important and interesting as the items included in the check list are the variants that may exist but that are not found in any word list because they are local in nature. One of the fascinating aspects of dialect study is the existence of these variants which make dialect mapping difficult and prevent any word list from being entirely complete. If you are alert to the possibility of finding variants not listed in the text, you may discover some interesting ones during your interviews with your informants. Carefully record these discoveries and report them to the class. In the course of discussion you may be able to determine the source of or reason for such variants.

When the check lists are returned to the class, a committee classifies and tabulates the results and finally reports findings concerning the dialectal terms most commonly used in the area and the regional background most influencing local speech. Of course, while the results of such a survey are somewhat indicative, they are too limited to be at all conclusive. However, your survey will give you an idea of how dialect information is gathered and you will very likely turn up some interesting facts about dialect in your own area.[1]

Compile Materials for Linguistic Investigation

As an example of the material an interviewer might use, write a series of questions designed to bring out differences in pronunciation, vocabulary, and grammar.

Contribute to a Language Study Bulletin Board

Collect materials to contribute to a classroom bulletin board featuring the study of language. Such items as news stories, headlines, editorials, cartoons, or advertisements may be posted under a decoratively lettered title or centered by an original cartoon. Posting materials as students bring them will keep the bulletin board news current and interesting.

---

[1] *Guide for High School English,* (Portland, Oregon, 1962), p. 303.

CHAPTER III

FORCES UNDERLYING DIALECT DISTRIBUTION IN THE U. S. A.

INTRODUCTION

The various regional surveys which make up the Linguistic Atlas of the United States clearly show that distinct dialect areas exist in our country. Now we wish to explain this fact and also to describe what these different areas are like. In order to do these two things, we must look at several parts of our country's history. Indeed, it becomes more and more apparent that the important facts about U. S. dialects are usually fairly firmly planted in our economic, social, and cultural history.

For purposes of discussion in this chapter, we shall divide this total historical background into 1) the nature of the thirteen original settlements, 2) the impact of the Westward Movement, and 3) the impact of the three social forces of the growth of industry, the growth of cities, and the spread of education.

THE THIRTEEN ORIGINAL COLONIES

The earliest settlers, who came with John Smith to Virginia, with Lord Calvert to Maryland, with Roger Williams to Rhode Island, with William Penn to Pennsylvania, with the Pilgrim Fathers and the Massachusetts Bay Company to Massachusetts, spoke Elizabethan English. At this time, the dialect of English spoken in London—Shakespeare's English—was in the process of becoming the accepted standard for the English-speaking world as a whole. In the early 1600's, however, when the first North American colonies were being founded, only about five percent of the world's five million English speakers used this London dialect. Outside of London, the English countryside was a patchwork of local dialects. Many of these local dialects crossed the Atlantic Ocean with the colonists and mixed in the speech of the earliest colonies. Communication among colonies was rare and difficult because of poor roads, great distances, hostile Indians, and political rivalries. Thus, even today, the clearest dialect boundaries in the U. S. A. are found along the coastal strip where the first settlements were located.

Expansion from these original coastal settlements was slow and difficult. Some of the newer settlements developed into important cities—Boston, New York, Philadelphia, Richmond, Charleston. It was not until after 1720, however, when large numbers of Ulster Scots arrived, that large-scale migration began across the Appalachian Mountains. The first crossing was made in Pennsylvania where, although the mountains were rugged, the Indians were friendly. Moving southwestward, these settlers populated the Shenandoah Valley, the inland areas of North and South Carolina, and Georgia. The dialect of these settlers is called "South Midland"; it differs from the language of the Southern colonists in important ways which will be explained later. Furthermore, the new settlers were yeoman farmers who did not sympathize with the plantation system of the Southerners. Even though these yeoman farmers were impressed by the culture of such important cities as Richmond, Charleston, and Savannah, they never surrendered their own basic way of life and viewpoint. This difference between yeoman farmer and Southern planter played an important part in American history because West Virginia broke away from Viriginia when Virginia seceded from the Union during the Civil War.

THE WESTWARD MOVEMENT

In general, the movement of pioneers from east to west across the North American continent extended the original settlement patterns of the Atlantic Seaboard. In the early days, the least important contributions were made by Eastern New England and the South. The former was tied to commerce and the sea, and it was not till about the middle of the nineteenth century that people of coastal New England played an important part in the exploration, settlement, and economic development of such Pacific Coast areas as those around San Francisco, the lower Columbia River, and Puget Sound.

The South of course was tied to the plantation system. Much of the new western territory was closed to slavery by Congress, and this fact restricted expansion of the plantation system. It is true that some plantation owners did migrate to the Gulf states, the lower Mississippi Valley, and east Texas, as we shall see later. Moreover, some private schools in the Middle West did import teachers from Eastern New England. However, these Southern and Eastern New England expansions were not nearly so important or widespread as those of settlers from Western New England, upstate New York, and Pennsylvania. The dialect of Western New England and upstate New York is called "Northern," whereas the dialect of Pennsylvania is called "Midland." We have already noted that one branch of Midland—South Midland—moved south with the migration of the yeomen farmers into the southern uplands after 1720. Later, South Midlanders migrated from Virginia and the Carolinas into Kentucky and then northward across the Ohio River into southern Ohio and Illinois and most of Indiana.

The other branch of Midland is called "North Midland." Although there was some movement of North Midlanders down the Allegheny River and then the Ohio River, most of the Pennsylvania speakers of the dialect traveled by inland transportation along the National Road. Such travel was much more difficult, dangerous, and expensive than moving by the water routes of the Great Lakes to the north or the Ohio River to the south. North Midland settlements in the West are found in a geographic wedge, broadest at its starting point in Pennsylvania and narrowest at the point where the borders of Illinois, Missouri, and Iowa meet.

Therefore, the most important sources of the population and consequently of the dialect of the Great Lakes area and the Mississippi Valley were 1) Western New England and the New York upstate communities springing from it, and 2) the southern uplands. Yankee settlers from New England and New York moved west by the Mohawk Valley and the Great Lakes, while the yeoman farmers of the South moved west by the Ohio River. Their settlement patterns in the West reflect their ways of life in the East. The yeoman farmers usually moved in family groups and chose low-lying ground near rivers where trees would grow. The Yankees moved in groups larger than the family—just as the Pilgrim Fathers had moved in 1620—and settled on the mighty prairies, which they mastered.

About 1840, large-scale emigration from northern Europe took place. Compact groups settled in both rural and urban areas of the North-Central States. Generally these settlers placed so high a value on education and learned English so immediately and so thoroughly that relatively few words from their native languages entered English.

In moving into the states of the "Inland South"—western Georgia, Tennessee, Alabama, Mississippi, Louisiana, Arkansas, Oklahoma— settlers from the Atlantic Seaboard seemed to advance toward the Southwest in a very irregular fashion. Treaties, the lure of good land, the presence of physical barriers, and opposition by Indians—all these forces combined to cause erratic changes of direction and pace in westward migration.

For instance, Georgians moving inland from the Atlantic Coast had established Augusta on the Savannah River by 1735. By 1775 they held an area between the Savannah and the Ogeechee Rivers that was two hundred miles long and, in some places, a hundred miles wide. Here their advance was stopped by the resistance of Cherokee and Creek Indians. Any Georgian who wanted land farther west had to cross the Indian barrier to join other pioneers who had come into newly occupied parts of Alabama and Mississippi by way of Tennessee.

The advance into Tennessee had been somewhat easier. By 1770 pioneers from Pennsylvania, Virginia, and other Atlantic Seaboard regions had moved southwest along the fertile Shenandoah Valley and other corridors until their settlements reached the upper part of the Holston River. Daniel Boone passed through these settlements on his way to the Cumberland Gap and Kentucky. A half-century later, pioneer families had established themselves in most of Kentucky and in eastern and central parts of Tennessee. An Indian barrier in western Tennessee deflected the pioneer advance southward. Settlers opened up the lands along the Alabama rivers all the way to the Gulf of Mexico. Then they moved across the lower part of Mississippi into Louisiana and, turning northwest, advanced along the rivers into Arkansas.

The settlement of Oklahoma shows another combination of forces influencing the patterns of settlement. After the War of 1812, complex developments led to an increasing production of cotton and a greater demand for the Indians' lands—either by purchase or by eviction. Within twenty years the Indians had been removed from southern lands and resettled in Oklahoma. There they blocked the southern advance to the West. In 1889 Congress forced the Indians to surrender their land rights in that territory, and Oklahoma was settled by land rushes. Oklahoma City gained a population of ten thousand persons overnight. These new settlers brought with them the vocabularies of adjacent northern, eastern, and southern localities.

Little is known about the earliest settlers in Texas, who came before she achieved her independence from Mexico in 1835. Of the soldiers who fought at the Battle of San Jacinto, on April 21, 1836, only twenty percent were born in states to the north of the Potomac and the Ohio Rivers. After independence, the greatest proportion of immigrants came through Alabama, Tennessee, Mississippi, Arkansas, Georgia, Louisiana, Missouri, and Kentucky.

Until the Civil War, the "Old South" contributed the leading group of Texas settlers—both in size and in social prestige—inasmuch as this group represented the earliest settlers. Of course many Negroes were brought to Texas and slavery flourished there until the Civil War. Today, however, the Negro population is concentrated in the eastern part of the state. If the planters moved farther west, their former slaves did not go with them.

Of the foreign elements in Texas, the earliest German migration came during the period of the Republic (1835-1845). German migration continued after the Civil War; settlers came from Prussia, Moravia, and Bohemia. Some of these settlers spoke Czech rather than German. The great majority of Latin Americans who live in Texas came during the late nineteenth and early twentieth centuries, principally from Mexico. The Latin population is still heavily concentrated in the southern and western extremities of the state.

Settlement of the Upper Midwest took place chiefly about the middle of the nineteenth century. Shortly before the Civil War, settlers from several main westward migration streams moved into Iowa and southern Minnesota. One group of settlers came from New England and upstate New York, or from Ohio, Michigan, Illinois, and Wisconsin—regions which had been settled earlier by New Englanders and New Yorkers. A second group came from the mid-Atlantic region, principally Pennsylvania, and from settlements established earlier by Pennsylvanians in Ohio, Indiana, and Illinois. A third group was part of the westward movement through the Cumberland Gap into Kentucky, southern Ohio, southern Illinois, and most of Indiana.

At the same time that these first English-speaking settlers were arriving in the Upper Midwest, the first immigrants from Europe settled throughout the entire area. They continued to arrive in increasing numbers and sometimes settled in compact communities and sometimes dispersed widely through the region. Most numerous were the Germans. They settled chiefly in Minnesota, Iowa, and Nebraska. The Scandinavians were numerous too—Norwegians, Swedes, Danes, Icelanders, and Finns. As a group they made up the largest foreign stock of Minnesota and the Dakotas. Many Hollanders settled in Iowa and in Minnesota. A second later wave of new immigrants from central and southern Europe followed the first influx of Germans, Scandinavians, and Hollanders. Czechs became farmers in Nebraska and western Minnesota; Poles, Hungarians, and Czechs became mine workers in northern Minnesota.

In the Rocky Mountains, rugged climate and hostile Indians and the gamble of mining operations made settlements spring up overnight and disappear as quickly. There was much movement of people. People from Kentucky and Missouri followed the mining booms to Montana. Cowboys moved constantly between west Texas and Wyoming. Spanish-Indian and Mormon settlements appeared in the Rockies. Thus the usual scattering and mixing of dialects was increased, as it were, by a constant crossbreeding of dialects. Terms from the Upper Midwest extend west into the Rocky Mountain area. Conversely, Western mountain and range terms extend eastward into the Upper Midwest. Denver shows a large Northern element. Utah too exhibits a preference for Northern terms.

In the last two decades, the Rocky Mountain States have vastly improved their natural attractiveness through better roads, new water power resources, new irrigation and mining projects. The result has been a steady increase in population, much of it inland from the Pacific Coast. Therefore the dialect situation in the Rocky Mountain States today is fluid, and the dialects of the Pacific Coast are doubly interesting—for themselves and for their influence on the Rocky Mountain area.

In the Westward Movement, the principal migration routes divided at the Rocky Mountains and continued westward in two separate directions. The Oregon Trail led northwestward toward the Oregon Territory, which included our present states of Oregon, Washington, Idaho, and a small part of western Montana. The California Trail led almost due west toward California. The population of the Pacific Coast states came from many sources. In fact, the dialect mixture makes it extremely difficult to establish isoglosses.

One interesting generalization can be made about California dialects, however. As Professor David Reed states it: ". . . the popularity of a word in California tends to reflect the generality of its distribution in Eastern dialects." That is, if a word is used everywhere, or almost everywhere, in the East, it will predominate over other possible variants in California. On the other hand, words that are used in limited areas of the East will be rare or nonexistent in California.

In Idaho and Washington, Northern settlers continued that dialect from Western New England, upstate New York, Michigan, Wisconsin, and Minnesota. Oregon, however, shows the Missouri influence by many Midland terms. The dialects of these areas also show the influence of German and Scandinavian immigrants.

California had, in addition, Spanish, French, Italian, Chinese, Japanese, Filipino, and Armenian immigrants. From the days of the Gold Rush till the early years of the twentieth century, upstate New Yorkers immigrated in great numbers to California, as did natives of Illinois, Missouri, and Iowa. In the early days before 1880, many New Englanders from Massachusetts and Maine were important new settlers in California, especially in the San Francisco Bay area. Natives of Pennsylvania and Ohio also immigrated to California throughout the settlement period. In the early 1930's dispossessed farmers from the dustbowl regions of Arkansas, Oklahoma, and Texas migrated to Southern California. This extreme mixture of population suggests that we might expect to find a highly diversified dialect mixture in California, and indeed this proves to be so. All areas are represented.

Thus we can see that the dialect patterns of the original settlements on the Atlantic Seaboard are reflected, more or less systematically, in the westward progress of the people's dialects across the continent. Futhermore, we observe that everywhere the influence of foreign language settlements is important.

SOCIAL FORCES

Finally, certain social forces influenced dialect distribution in the U. S. A. These are 1) the growth of industry, 2) the growth of cities, and 3) the spread of education.

1. The Growth of Industry

The Industrial Revolution began in England shortly before the American Revolution separated the colonies from the mother country. In America, industries developed quickly after the colonies became independent. A tariff protected the infant industries. Unlimited resources of nature and human energy encouraged the growth of industries. They in turn could readily market their products because the population was rapidly expanding. There was plenty of work for everybody, and more and more immigrants sought jobs in industry rather than in farming.

2. The Growth of Cities

Cities were the natural result of industrialization. In 1775 many large cities already existed in America. Philadelphia, Boston, New York, and Charleston were especially important. The Erie Canal—opened to Great Lakes shipping in 1830—and the railroads stimulated the growth of more cities. Fleeing from revolutions and other disasters in Europe, Germans, Hungarians, Poles, Irish, Scandinavians, and Italians emigrated to the U. S. A. to work in industry and business. Centering around oil refineries and steel and textile mills, other great cities have sprung up. Today, the majority of Americans live in cities. Our culture is basically urban, no longer rural. The speech forms of the cities are replacing those of the rural areas. Indeed, the great cities have mighty cultural prestige and are strong forces in shaping regional types of speech.

3. The Spread of Education

Education is probably the strongest single force for removing local and regional dialect expressions. This fact is especially true if we consider travel as a form of education. When young men join the armed forces, they travel. The soldier from interior Tennessee who says, "I hope how soon I'll get a furlough," soon learns that few people outside his small community say, "I hope how soon."

If we consider television as another form of education, we realize two points. First, television uses local dialects for realistic or humorous effects. The dialect of the marshal of a small western town is as much a part of him as his ten-gallon hat and his six-shooters. The dialect of the family that moves from Mississippi to Maine is looked upon as humorous by the Yankees. Second, the dialect of the network newscaster can be understood by everybody in the United States. Furthermore, it is often copied by listeners and therefore helps to smooth out regional dialect differences.

Education in the narrower sense of schools, books, and newspapers has been important in America since the beginning of our history. Harvard College was established in 1636. Puritans had to know how to read in order to understand their Bibles, and in the southern colonies also literacy was high. The Northwest Ordinance of 1787 set aside public land in the West for the support of education. Indeed, since we lack any firmly established aristocracy, education has become the passport to social and economic advancement. With education, the standard language becomes second nature, either replacing or submerging local dialect forms.

SUMMARY

We have now examined the most important forces that underlie the distribution of dialects throughout the United States. We have noted how our history has combined with geography and the desire for new and better opportunities to spread the original dialect patterns of the Atlantic Seaboard settlements all the way to the Pacific Coast. We have then seen that three great economic forces—industrialization, urbanization, and education—have worked to change and often to erase regional speech and to produce a more uniform kind of American English.

SUGGESTIONS FOR STUDY

Map Dialect Distribution in Your State

On an outline map of your state indicate the way in which movements of groups of people and the impact of social forces have influenced dialect distribution in your state.

Test Your Comprehension

1. Name the aspects of history and the social forces that have influenced dialect distribution in the United States.

2. What type of English speech did the earliest colonists bring to New England and the South?

3. What factors prevented the dialects of Eastern New England and the South from spreading as rapidly as those of Western New England, upstate New York, and Pennsylvania?

4. Name the three main dialect areas originating in the eastern part of the United States.

5. Name and discuss factors influencing the dialects used in the speech of the Pacific Coast.

6. Discuss the dialects used in the Rocky Mountain States, explaining early influences and accounting for the occurrence of Pacific Coast dialects in this region.

7. In what way has the spread of education tended to encourage the breaking down of dialectal boundaries?

Add to Your Vocabulary

Using the dictionary make sure of the meaning of these words: *yeoman, migration,* and *literacy.* For each one write a headline as it might appear above a news story featuring the word.

Listen to Records

The "Spoken English" record album which accompanies the *Guide to Modern English* for grades 9 and 10 includes a demonstration of dialect differences in the United States. This program, which is presented by Henry Lee Smith, Jr., is the only part of the album suitable for dialect study.

American Dialect Recordings (The Linguaphone Institute) also demonstrate dialect.

Recordings made of the musical comedy, *My Fair Lady,* offer standard British dialect in the part taken by Rex Harrison as well as cockney dialect in the songs sung by Stanley Holloway. Recordings of their own poems read by such American and British poets as Carl Sandburg and Dylan Thomas afford an interesting listening experience.

Write a Report

Choose one of the forces contributing to the distribution of language in the United States to study and develop in a written report. Suggestions might include a study of the use of dialect in television programs; the influence on the surrounding area of one large city in your state; one migration westward (the time, type of people, place of origin in Europe and on the Eastern seaboard, eventual place of settlement); or the characteristics of Elizabethan English. Supply a bibliography. You might combine this study with a project in social studies.

CHAPTER IV

THE MAIN DIALECT AREAS OF THE U. S. A.

INTRODUCTION

The most important single contribution of Atlas research to our knowledge of present-day American English is Professor Hans Kurath's definition of the three major dialect areas of the eastern U. S. A. This definition was first published in his *A Word Geography of the Eastern United States* in 1949. This book was based on the atlases of New England, and the Middle and South Atlantic States.

By means of strong dialect boundaries—closely knit bundles of isoglosses—showing consistent pronunciations, vocabulary, and grammar, Kurath described the Northern, the Midland, and the Southern dialect areas. Later research for the other regional atlases has shown that these same dialect divisions can be traced across the continent to the Pacific Coast. The farther west we go, the more overlapping and mingling of dialects we find. However, with sufficient knowledge of the history of our country, its geography, and dialect field work, the areas can be interestingly charted.

In this chapter, these three major dialect areas will be discussed. For each in turn, first its geographic extent will be stated, and then its typical dialect characteristics will be defined in terms of pronunciation, vocabulary, and grammar.

THE NORTHERN DIALECT AREA

On the Atlantic Seaboard, the Northern dialect area includes New England, the Hudson Valley, upstate New York, the northernmost strip of Pennsylvania, and Greater New York City. Moving westward into the area covered by the Atlas of the North-Central States, we find the inland Northern area which includes Michigan, Wisconsin, the northern counties of Ohio, Indiana, Illinois, and Iowa. Still farther west, in the Upper Midwest Atlas area, the Northern dialect appears in Minnesota, North Dakota, the northern third of Iowa, and the northeastern half of South Dakota. In this area, there is some mingling of dialect forms so

that the lines of separation between Northern and Midland are harder
to draw. Apparently, in the Upper Midwest, the Northern dialect is
contracting and the Midland is expanding. Farther west, in the Rocky
Mountain States, only Colorado has been thoroughly studied. Here
Denver and Gunnison are "islands" of Northern dialect. There is other
evidence, too, of Northern forms in Colorado. However, overlapping of
Northern and Midland dialects is the rule in this state. Utah generally
shows a preference for Northern terms although the southern part of
that state shows some Midland usage. Western Montana shows a North-
ern-Midland mixture. In the Pacific Northwest, Washington and northern
and eastern Idaho are predominantly Northern in dialect. Preliminary
editing of the California material shows that many words from Northern
dialect areas in the East and Great Lakes region occur in California.

Typical Northern pronunciation items are:

Contrast between /o/ and /ɔ/ in the pairs:[1]
    mourning and morning I, II, III.
    hoarse and *horse* I, II, III.
    fourteen and *forty* I, II, III.
/ɨ/ in the unstressed syllable of *haunted* and *careless* I, II, III.
/ð/ regularly in *with* I, II, III.
/s/ in *grease* (verb) and *greasy* (adjective) I, II, III.
/bɨkəz/ *because* I, II, III.

Typical Northern vocabulary items are:
    pail (Midland and Southern *bucket*) I, II, III.
    clapboards 'finished siding' (Midland and Southern *weather-
        boards* and *weatherboarding*) I, II, III.
    brook 'small stream' I, II, III.
    cherry pit 'cherry seed' I, II, III.
    angleworm 'earthworm' I, II, III.
    johnnycake 'cornbread' I, II, III.
    eaves trough 'gutter on roof' I, II, [III].
    spider 'frying pan' I, II.

Typical Northern grammar items are:
    dove as past tense of *dive* I, II, III.
    sick to the stomach I, II, [III].
    he isn't to home 'he isn't at home' I, II.
    hadn't ought 'oughtn't' I, II.

---

[1]The Roman numerals after each item state the type of informants who charac-
teristically use the item, as explained in Chapter II, page 12. When these Roman
numerals are enclosed in brackets, less currency in that group is indicated.

clim as past tense of *climb*   I, II.

be as a finite verb   (*How be you?* for 'How are you?')   I.

scairt 'scared'   I, II.

THE MIDLAND DIALECT AREA

On the Atlantic Seaboard, the Midland dialect area includes central and southern Pennsylvania, northern Delaware, and the areas of Pennsylvania settlement on the Delaware, Susquehanna, and upper Ohio Rivers. It extends south into the Shenandoah Valley, the southern Appalachians, and the upper Piedmont of North and South Carolina. Moving westward to the North-Central States area, we find North Midland forms (and Midland forms) in central Ohio, central and northern Indiana, and central Illinois. South Midland forms (and Midland forms) occur in Kentucky and the areas settled by Kentuckians in southern Ohio, southern Indiana, and southern Illinois. Furthermore, because of migrations north on the Mississippi River, South Midland forms are found also in the mining regions of northwestern Illinois, southwestern Wisconsin, and southern Iowa.

The Upper Midwest also shares in this expansion north of the Midland dialect. Midland forms are found in all the states of the Upper Midwest Atlas area and South Midland forms in all except North Dakota. Farther west, in Colorado, we find competition between the Midland and the Northern dialects. Probably, however, Midland is Colorado's basic usage. Upon this early and continuing base, apparently, certain Northern features have been superimposed. In the Pacific Northwest, Oregon and western and southern Idaho show a preference for Midland forms, though there is a great and confusing overlapping which has not yet been completely analyzed. In California, Midland terms are as frequent and as widely distributed as Northern forms are.

In Texas the vocabulary is predominantly Midland and Southern, with purely Southern terms in a minority. Apparently Texas pronunciation, as far as it has been studied, shows definitely South Midland characteristics in the northern and western parts of the state.

In the Inland South, Midland and South Midland vocabulary items seem to form a distribution pattern which vaguely resembles a T. The top of the T goes along the northern borders of Tennessee, Arkansas, and Oklahoma, and expands southward into these states and into northern Mississippi and northwestern Georgia. The stem of the T goes south through Alabama to the Gulf of Mexico, bounded by the Chattahoochie River on the east and the Tombigbee River on the west. On the other hand, certain features of pronunciation suggest that the basic Midland-

Southern dialect boundary across Alabama may lie just north of Montgomery. Until field interviews are conducted and furnish more evidence on the dialect situation in the Inland South, these two types of evidence are both of great interest to the student of dialect geography.

Typical Midland pronunciation items are:

/r/ kept after vowels I, II, III.
/ɔ/ in *on;* /ɔh/ in *wash* and *wasp;* /ɔw/ in *hog, frog,* and *fog* I, II, III.
[ɛ] in *Mary* and *dairy* I, II, III.
/ə/ in the unstressed syllable of *haunted* and *careless* I, II, III.
/θ/ regularly in *with* I, II, III.
/r/ frequently intruding in *wash* and *Washington* I, II.

Typical Midland vocabulary items are:

a little piece 'a short distance' I, II, III.
blinds 'window shades' I, II, III.
skillet 'frying pan' I, II, III.
snake feeder 'dragon fly' I, II, [III].
poke 'paper sack' I, II, [III].
green beans 'string beans' I, II, III.
to hull beans 'to shell beans' I, II, [III].
spouts, spouting 'eaves troughs' I, II, [III].

Typical Midland grammar items are:

all the further 'as far as' I, II.
I'll wait on you 'I'll wait for you' I, II, [III].
I want off 'I want to get off' I, II, [III].
quarter till eleven I, II, III.

THE SOUTHERN DIALECT AREA

On the Atlantic Seaboard, the Southern dialect area includes Delmarvia (the Eastern Shore of Maryland and Virginia, and southern Delaware). It extends southward into the Virginia Piedmont, northeastern North Carolina, eastern South Carolina, Georgia, and Florida. Along the Gulf Coast, Southern forms appear in central and southern Mississippi and thoughout Louisiana and Texas. In *The Regional Vocabulary of Texas,* Professor Atwood says, "I have no hesitation in classing virtually all of Texas and an indeterminate portion of the surrounding states as a major branch of General Southern, which I will label *Southwestern.*" It contains Southern, Midland, and Southwestern words. In the North-Central States, only Kentucky shows Southern forms —especially western Kentucky—since that state has always been somewhat dependent culturally on Tidewater and Piedmont Virginia. Southern forms are relatively rare in California and practically absent in the Pacific Northwest as well as in other Northern dialect areas.

Typical Southern pronunciation items are:

/r/ lost except before vowels I, II, III.
/ey/ in *Mary* I, II, III.
/ɨ/ in unstressed syllables of *haunted* and *careless* I, II, III.
/ɨl/ in *towel* and *funnel;* /ɨn/ in *mountain* I, II, [III].
/z/ in *Mrs.* [I], II, III.

Typical Southern vocabulary items are:

low 'moo' I, II, III.
carry 'escort, take' I, II, [III].
snap beans, snaps 'string beans' I, II, III.
harp, mouth harp 'harmonica' I, II, III.
turn of wood 'armload of wood' I, II, [III].
fritters I, II, III.

Typical Southern grammar items are:

it wan't me I, II, [III].
he belongs to be careful I, II.
he fell outn the bed I.
all two, all both 'both' I, [II].
on account of 'because' I, [II].

SUMMARY

Although much more work has to be done to finish mapping the dialects of the United States, enough is now known so that we can make certain broad generalizations about our country's speech. The most important of these generalizations is that three different dialect bands extend from east to west across the U. S. A. These dialects are named Northern, Midland, and Southern. They are defined by means of differences in pronunciation, vocabulary, and grammar. On the Atlantic Seaboard, they reflect the patterns of original settlement. Farther inland, they reflect later migrations of people. The more recently settled the area, the less clearly defined are its patterns of dialect distribution.

These important conclusions wipe out earlier notions that something called "General American" speech exists. This supposed speech type is usually defined as extending from New Jersey on the Atlantic Coast through the Middle West and the entire Pacific Coast. Nor does a Midwestern dialect as such exist. Clearly, such descriptions of dialects in the U. S. A. are vastly oversimplified.

Another interesting fact revealed by the Atlas investigations is that dialect areas do not match up with state lines. Indeed, dialects show practically no respect for man-made boundaries. They are deeper and stronger than such divisions.

SUGGESTIONS FOR STUDY

Chart the Major Language Areas of the United States

Beginning with the eastern seaboard and showing the spread of dialect westward to the Pacific Coast, chart and label the three major dialect areas on a map of the United States.

Test Your Comprehension

1. What important contribution has Professor Hans Kurath's *A Word Geography of the Eastern United States* made to the study of our language?
2. Name the three most clearly defined dialect areas in the country.
3. On the Atlantic Seaboard what states are included in each of these major dialect areas?
4. Why do we find increasing evidence of the overlapping and mingling of dialects as we trace their distribution westward?
5. Look again at the dialect word lists supplied in this chapter. Can you add any items? Can you supply any distinctly local variants?

Add to Your Vocabulary

Find each of the following words in the text: *cultural, generalization,* and *superimpose*. Copy each in context into your language notebook; add the dictionary meaning; and finally, use each one in a sentence in such a way that the meaning is clear.

Lead a Class Discussion

Prepare five questions based on the information provided in Chapter IV. Use these in leading a class discussion of the major language areas in the United States. Three students might work together, with each one conducting the discussion of the section of the chapter for which he is responsible.

This project can be expanded to constitute a review of the entire text to this point in preparation for an evaluation of the learning accomplished during the first part of the language study. In this case, students may work singly or in small groups to prepare questions and lead class discussion.

Point Out Dialect Boundaries

Study the map in the text that shows major dialect boundaries, and be ready to point out to the class the dialect areas and to indicate the spread of dialects on a wall map of the United States.

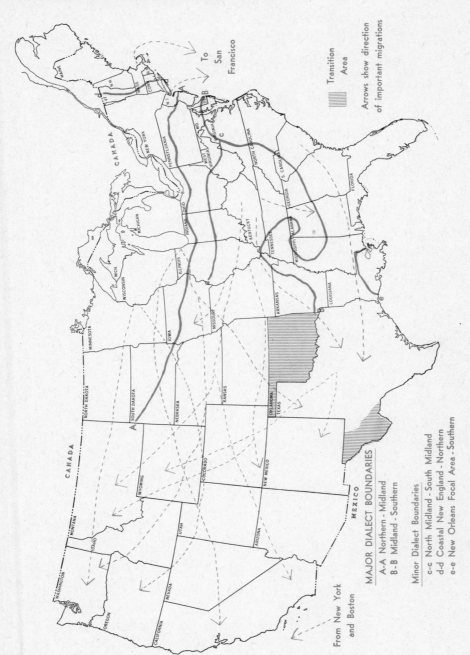

To San Francisco

Transition Area

Arrows show direction of important migrations

MAJOR DIALECT BOUNDARIES
A-A Northern - Midland
B-B Midland - Southern

Minor Dialect Boundaries
c-c North Midland - South Midland
d-d Coastal New England - Northern
e-e New Orleans Focal Area - Southern

From New York and Boston

CHAPTER V

THE INFLUENCE OF FOREIGN LANGUAGE SETTLEMENTS

INTRODUCTION

The United States has often been called the "Great Melting Pot." This name refers to our ability to absorb the many migrations of peoples from other countries into our own. In earlier years we welcomed immigrants and usually permitted them to settle where they wished.

In their new homes sometimes they retained their native language even while learning English. They used their native tongue within their own group and spoke English when they needed to communicate with persons outside their own immigrant group. More often, however, English overwhelmed their native language. Then they would speak English inside their own group as well as outside it. Nevertheless, their native language always left its marks upon the American English of the area where they had settled. These marks sometimes were in pronunciation or grammar, but most often they were in vocabulary, especially in the names of food. The prestige of English, however, was very great. This prestige was increased by the schools; almost all teaching was done in English. Moreover, compulsory universal education was the rule in the U. S. A. from very early days.

One notable exception to this rule of the supremacy of English was the Pennsylvania Germans, the so-called "Pennsylvania Dutch." This closely knit group of immigrants managed to maintain their own language for quite a long time. About 1700, the Pennsylvania Germans (Mennonites and Amish) migrated from the Rhineland Palatinate into Pennsylvania. They have maintained their Pennsylvania way of life to this day, and their language has contributed many vocabulary items to American English. Probably the best known is *smear case* or *smear cheese*, their name for cottage cheese. Others are *fat-cakes* 'doughnuts,' *hex* 'to cast a spell,' *rainworm* 'earthworm,' and *sauerkraut*.

THE COLONIAL PERIOD

In addition to the contributions of the Palatinate Germans, several other foreign language groups affected English in the Colonial period. The most important were the Algonquian Indians, the Africans, the New Amsterdam Dutch, and the French.

The Indians

When the earliest settlers arrived on the North American continent, they found plants and animals that did not exist in Europe. Since these new plants and animals had been given names by the Indians, the early settlers often took over these names intact and introduced them into English. Such words are called "loanwords." Although there were many Indian languages in America and they were subdivided into many dialects, the early settlers in both Virginia and Massachusetts met principally the Indians who belonged to the Algonquian group of tribes. The tribes within this group were many, but fortunately their languages were related.

From this language group come many animal names. *Opossum, moose, skunk, terrapin, woodchuck,* and *caribou* are examples. Many familiar plant names have the same kind of source. *Hickory, pecan, squash,* and *persimmon* are examples. Futhermore, the early settlers learned about Indian foods, customs, relationships, and artifacts, and adopted their names into English. Examples are: *hominy, succotash, johnnycake, pone, pemmican, moccasin, tomahawk, totem, wigwam, powwow, mackinaw, toboggan, wampum, papoose,* and *squaw.*

The Africans

More than a year before the Pilgrims landed on Plymouth Rock, a group of people were brought to North America against their will and sold into slavery. Along the coast of South Carolina and Georgia, both on the Sea Islands and the mainland, there are isolated communities of Negro Americans who cultivate rice, cotton, and indigo. They speak a dialect of English that has been so strongly influenced by the languages of Africa, which their ancient ancestors spoke, that it is not easily understood by other Americans.

This language is called Gullah. It has only recently been thoroughly studied. Although its contribution is not overly large, it is extremely interesting, especially because of the modern importance of African languages as new African nations achieve independence. English words of Gullah origin include *banjo, goober* 'peanut,' *cooter* 'turtle,' *juke, hoodoo* 'to bring bad luck to someone,' and *voodoo* 'magic.'

The Amsterdam Dutch

Relations between the New Amsterdam Dutch and the English colonists were not very friendly. Nevertheless, from the Dutch settlements of the area that is now New York City we have such vocabulary items as *coleslaw, cooky, bowery* (now a street name, but in New Amsterdam a farm), *pit* 'fruit stone,' *boodle, Santa Claus, waffle,* and probably *Yankee.*

The French

The French settled in America as early as the English did. Their language is spoken today in Quebec and in southwestern Louisiana. Before the Revolution, it contributed only a few words like *prairie, chowder, buccaneer,* and *calumet.*

THE POST-REVOLUTIONARY PERIOD

After 1800, English adopted many words from the Indians, the Spanish, the French, the Germans (both from the German language itself and from Yiddish), the Scandinavians, the Italians, the Chinese, and the Japanese. We shall discuss each in turn.

The Indians

As the pioneers moved west, western Indian words entered American English. For instance, the Dakotas gave us *tepee* and the Navahos gave us *hogan* to add to other names for Indian living places like *wigwam.* Cherokee supplied *sequoia* 'a kind of cone-bearing tree.' Chinook supplied the word *chinook* 'a warm dry wind in the Rocky Mountain region,' or a kind of salmon.

The Spanish

When the pioneers reached California, they found a language which was a blending of Spanish and Nahuatl, the language of the Aztecs. From this source, many words came into English: *coyote, chili, mesquite, avocado, tamale,* and *ocelot,* for examples. Other words that are common in Texas and adjoining parts of the Southwest seem to come more directly from Spanish itself. Some examples are: *arroyo* 'stream bed, usually dry,' *mesa* 'high flat land,' *vaquero* 'cowboy,' *mustang, ranch, adobe, senorita, peon, patio, tortilla, lasso, canyon, lariat, plaza, frijole, corral, bonanza, eldorado, fiesta, siesta,* and *padre.*

The French

With the Louisiana Purchase in 1803 and the settlement of the Mississippi Valley and the Great Lakes region, many French words entered English. Some of these are: *butte, chute, coulee* 'deep gulch,' *depot* 'railroad station,' and *picayune* 'an insignificant person or thing.' The word *shivaree*, from the French *charivari*, is especially interesting. It replaced the Western New England and upstate New York word *horning* as the name of the noisy burlesque serenade for a bride and groom just after their wedding. Today the word *shivaree* is heard throughout the Mississippi Valley from Minnesota and Wisconsin through Louisiana and west of the Mississippi to California.

The Germans

Political upheavals in Germany in 1848 caused the emigration of great numbers of Germans to the large cities of the Middle Atlantic States and to the farms and big cities of the Midwest. New York, Chicago, St. Louis, Cleveland, and Detroit, for instance. all had large groups of German settlers. The migration slowed down again with the return of prosperity after the Franco-Prussian War (1870), but this new influx of Germans contributed many loanwords to American English. Many of these concern food and drink: *rathskeller, bierstube, weinstube, lager, bock, delicatessen, wienerwurst, frankfurter, hamburger, schnitzel, pumpernickel, sauerbraten, pretzel, zwieback.*

From German borrowings we can learn also about "loanblends" and "loanshifts." From the loan word *hamburger* many loanblends have been created: *cheeseburger, chickenburger, turkeyburger, nutburger, wimpyburger, onionburger, beefburger, shrimpburger,* and others. A loanblend, therefore, is a combination of a borrowed word element with a native American English word to form a new word.

On the other hand, examples of loanshifts are the English version, *beer garden*, of the German *bier garten*, or the English *dumb*, meaning "stupid," for the German *dumm*, also meaning "stupid." In these loanshifts, we see English word elements which closely resemble the German word elements being substituted for them to form the new English words.

In connection with German loans, we shall consider Yiddish borrowings. Yiddish is basically German, with a large number of words borrowed from Hebrew and Slavic. However, not all the speakers of Yiddish came from Germany; many came from Poland and Russia. They settled in greatest numbers in New York City, and it is there that Yiddish borrowings are most numerous. Typical examples of Yiddish loanwords that are known throughout the U. S. A. are *kibitzer* 'giver of unwanted advice,' *schmalz* (or *schmaltz*) 'extremely sentimental music' (the word means "melted fat" in Yiddish), *schnozzle* 'big nose,' *phooey*, an exclamation of disgust or shame.

Possibly Al Capp got the name for his miraculous and lovable schmoo from the Yiddish *shmo*. In a radio talk Capp said that he picked the name because its sounds were very expressive, but it is possible that he may have been helped by having heard the Yiddish *shmo*.

Some of the Yiddish contributions to English are more clearly of Hebrew and Slavic than of German origin. *Kosher* is of Hebrew origin as are *goy* 'a gentile,' *Yehudi* 'a Jew,' *matzoth* 'cakes of unleavened bread,' *bar mizvah* 'a boy of thirteen, the age for assuming religious responsibilities,' and the Jewish holidays *Yom Kippur* and *Rosh Hashana*. *Borscht* (or *borsch*) 'sour beet soup' is Russian but transmitted through Yiddish into American English. *Gefilte fisch* 'stuffed fish' also comes in through Yiddish cookery.

The Scandinavians

During the last few years of the nineteenth century, large numbers of Scandinavians settled in the upper Mississippi Valley. Today Scandinavian language groups are located in the northern states from Michigan to the Pacific Coast and also in Illinois and Iowa. Most of the Scandinavians settled in rural communities, but several fairly large groups located in Cleveland, Chicago, and Brooklyn. Many Scandinavian words are used within these groups, but *smorgasbord* is probably the best known loanword throughout the U. S. A.

The Italians

Although many Italians have emigrated to the United States, their contributions to American English are few. Examples are: *macaroni, spaghetti, pizza, spumoni, minestrone, antipasto,* and *ravioli*.

The Chinese and Japanese

Settling principally on the Pacific Coast, the Chinese and Japanese have contributed few words to American English. From Chinese come *chow mein, chop suey, subgum, tong* 'Chinese secret society in the United States.' From Japanese come *hara-kiri, jujitsu, nisei* 'native-born American of Japanese parentage,' *issei* 'Japanese-born resident of the United States,' and *kibei* 'American-born person of Japanese parentage who goes to Japan for education.'

SUMMARY

These then are the most important foreign languages from which American English has borrowed and adapted words. It is an important fact about English that it loves to borrow words from other languages and has been doing so for the fifteen centuries of its development in all parts of the world. Furthermore, any language with which English has had contact anywhere in the world has left its trace upon our language. This habit of English does much to explain the wealth and diversity of our English vocabulary.

SUGGESTIONS FOR STUDY

Identify the Foreign Language Settlements in Your State

List in your language notebook the names and locations of the foreign language settlements in your state or section of the country, or locate these groups on a state or regional map.

Test Your Comprehension

1. Name the foreign language groups that contributed words to American English in the Colonial period.

2. Mention several of the foreign language groups that influenced our language in Post-Revolutionary times.

3. Define the following terms: *Pennsylvania Dutch, loanblend, loanshift, succotash, hogan,* and *chowder.*

4. Discuss in general terms the value to our language of the contributions made by foreign language groups.

Add to Your Vocabulary

Select five words from those of foreign origin listed in the text. You may choose these from one group, as, for example, terms used for foods, animals, or geographical features, or from different groups. After looking up the meaning, write a narrative paragraph using all five words.

Prepare and Give an Expository Speech

From your supplementary reading gather information for a speech that will bring to the attention of other members of the class some of the materials available for the study of language. Listed below are some ideas for reports together with references.

Early borrowings from the Indians; later borrowings from the Indians, especially in the West; borrowings from the Dutch, German, and Swedish; from the Yiddish; from the French, Spanish, and Italian; from the Chinese and Japanese; early American coinages; the unusual history of ten common words (see the dictionary references); the variety of meanings found in ten common words as these are used in different areas; the speechways of one state (or more than one where information is limited); characteristics of American pronunciation; ways in which America invents new words; the origin and nature of slang; a comparison of American and British vocabulary.

Among the references listed in the bibliography at the end of this text, the student will find especially helpful the following: *A Word Geography of the Eastern United States* by Hans Kurath; *The American*

Language, An Inquiry into the Development of English in the United States by H. L. Mencken; and *Words and Ways of American English* by Thomas Pyles. Also useful will be the two *Supplements* to the text by H. L. Mencken, already mentioned. These were published in 1945 and 1948. Two dictionaries which give examples of American usages of words are *The Dictionary of Americanisms,* edited by Mitford M. Mathews, and *The Dictionary of American English,* edited by Sir William Craigie and James R. Hulbert. The exploration of the meanings of such words as the following can be a fascinating study: *apple-sauce, canoe, corduroy, diamond, geoduck, hex, loggerhead, overalls, quirt, rambunctious, salamander, van, wapatoo, Yankee,* and *zigzag.*

SELECTED BIBLIOGRAPHY ON LINGUISTIC GEOGRAPHY

Allen, Harold B., ed. "Linguistic Geography," *Readings in Applied English Linguistics.* New York: Appleton-Century-Crofts, 1958.

Anderson, Wallace L., and Norman G. Stageberg, eds. "Linguistic Geography," *Introductory Readings on Language.* New York: Holt, Rinehart & Winston, Inc., 1962.

Atwood, E. Bagby. *A Survey of Verb Forms in the Eastern United States.* Ann Arbor: University of Michigan Press, 1953.

_____. *The Regional Vocabulary of Texas.* Austin: University of Texas Press, 1962.

Bloomfield, Leonard. "Dialect Geography," *Language.* New York: Holt, Rinehart & Winston, Inc., 1933.

de Saussure, Ferdinand. "Geographical Linguistics," *Course in General Linguistics.* Translated from the French by Wade Baskin. New York: Philosophical Library, 1959.

Gleason, H. A., Jr. "Variations in Speech," *An Introduction to Descriptive Linguistics,* Revised Edition. New York: Holt, Rinehart & Winston, Inc., 1961.

Hall, Robert A., Jr. "Language Covers Territory," *Linguistics and Your Language.* New York: Doubleday & Company, Inc. (paperback: Anchor A201).

Hockett, Charles F. "Dialect Geography," *A Course in Modern Linguistics.* New York: Macmillan Company, 1958.

Ives, Sumner. "A Theory of Literary Dialect," *Tulane Studies in English,* II (New Orleans, 1950), pp. 137-182.

Kurath, Hans, and others. *Handbook of the Linguistic Geography of New England.* Washington: American Council of Learned Societies, 1939.

_____. *A Word Geography of the Eastern United States*. Ann Arbor: University of Michigan Press, 1949.

_____, and Raven I. McDavid, Jr. *The Pronunciation on English in the Atlantic States*. Ann Arbor: University of Michigan Press, 1961.

Marckwardt, Albert H. *American English*. New York: Oxford University Press, 1959.

McDavid, Raven I., Jr. "The Dialects of American English," in W. Nelson Francis, *The Structure of American English*. New York: Ronald Press, 1958.

Mencken, H. L. "The Common Speech," *The American Language, An Inquiry into the Development of English in the United States*, Fourth Edition. New York: Alfred A. Knopf, Inc., 1936.

Pyles, Thomas. *Words and Ways of American English*. New York: Random House, 1952.

Reed, Carroll E. *American Dialects*. Seattle: University of Washington Press, 1958.

CHAPTER VI
DIALECT IN LITERATURE

Dialect has long been used in literature for many different artistic purposes. Aristophanes used it in ancient Greece. Chaucer and Shakespeare used it in England. By it they could say many subtle things about their characters. For instance, they could place a person in a certain social class or in a certain geographic region, or both. They could create funny effects, drawing easy laughter from their audiences by using the speaker of a nonstandard dialect as a foil for his betters. They could also create insights by showing the speaker of dialect as a pure and undefiled child of nature. Likewise, in the United States, writers like Mark Twain, Joel Chandler Harris, and James Russell Lowell have used dialect to add color, to bring out contrasts among their characters, or to add a comic touch to their writing.

However, the problems in using dialect are rather complex. Speech is oral, and writing can never do more than suggest its variety and complexity. The dialect writer is limited to the symbols of standard spelling and punctuation. Obviously, these are insufficient to report dialectal differences fully and accurately. Thus the dialect writer is always forced to compromise and to seek the best way to represent the differences which will make the character distinctive and realistic without making his speech unreadable.

For example, Joel Chandler Harris, in writing the Negro dialect of the famous Uncle Remus stories, uses phonetic devices like *d* for *th* in *the, that, them,* and *whether,* and *f* for *th* in words like *mouth* and *tooth.* He writes *before* as *befo',* *surely* as *sholy,* and *poor* as *po'.* In the dialect areas of vocabulary and grammar, he lets Uncle Remus invent words like *sollumsholly, sustonished,* and *rekermember,* expressions like *leg-bail* for "escape by flight," and *You're thumpin' de wrong wattermillion* for "you're barking up the wrong tree," proverbs like *'ooman tongue ain't got no Sunday,* and comparisons like *ez ca'm ez a dead pig in de sunshine.*

Such use of dialect is more skillful than another common kind of imitation speech called "eye dialect." This is a falsely phonetic respelling of ordinary words to suggest a nonstandard pronunciation. It is false in that it does not really reflect anything unusual in the pronunciation of these words. To spell common words like *because, women, was,* and *says,* as *bekuz, wimmin, wuz,* and *sez* actually records the standard English pronunciation of these words. This kind of misspelling is very common in comics and other inaccurate representations of American dialects. It is also present to a greater or less degree in all the dialect literature we are considering here. However, in no case do the authors of this literature rely exclusively upon eye dialect to represent the speech of their characters. They generally resist the natural tendency to use eye dialect to exaggerate the dialectal differences of their ignorant or illiterate characters.

Another difficulty in writing and interpreting literary dialect lies in the very nature of the dialect situation in the United States. Each author himself speaks some one regional variety of Northern, Midland, or Southern dialect. Many of the regional features of any dialect are common to all levels of culture and education within the area. An author probably often will not even be conscious that such features are "dialectal." They will not seem so to him.

For example, a writer from Georgia, Virginia, or Eastern New England will not think that his "r-less" pronunciation of *water* is dialectal, even though he may know that Missourians generally pronounce this word with a strong *r* ending. Nor will an author from Missouri recognize his pronunciation of *water* as dialectal in spite of the fact that he pronounces the word as *warter,* with an internal *r* sound in addition to his strong *r* ending. Neither author would see any need to change the standard spelling of the word *water* to indicate his own pronunciation of it. He naturally considers that this standard spelling faithfully represents his pronunciation of the word.

Therefore it is to be expected that an author will not represent features of his characters' speech if they are not perceived as dialectal in his own dialect. Furthermore, the letters he uses to spell pronunciations will differ in phonetic reference in different dialect areas. A Southern writer, for instance, will spell his pronunciation of *I* and *my* with those standard spellings, but a Northern or Midland author would spell the Southerner's pronunciation of these words as *ah* or *mah.* These spellings represent the "Southern dialect" to the Northern or Midland speaker. In order for the reader of dialect literature to interpret these spellings accurately he must know something of the author's native dialect. If it is the same as his own, no problem exists. Otherwise, misunderstandings are likely unless one has travelled widely or studied American dialects carefully.

Ordinarily, the speech of educated persons is not represented in "dialectal respelling" by authors who are portraying their own region. All educated characters are depicted as speaking standard English, properly spelled. However, since there is no national spoken standard, but only regional standards, we can assume that standard spelling means that the character speaks according to the generally accepted standards for educated speakers in his own region.

With these introductory comments, the following bibliography of dialect literature is presented. The different selections should be read and interpreted in the light of the dialect information discussed in this chapter.

LITERARY SELECTIONS ILLUSTRATING AMERICAN DIALECTS

POEMS

Benét, Stephen Vincent.   "The Mountain Whippoorwill"   (Georgia)

Dunbar, Paul L.   "The Turning of the Babies in the Bed"
"A Coquette Conquered"   (Uneducated Southern Negro)

Field, Eugene.   "Seein' Things"
and others   (Midwest)

Frost, Robert.   "Death of the Hired Man"
and other dialogues and monologues   (New England)

Furman, Lucy.   "Ballad of Kents and Fallons"   (Kentucky Mountains)

Helton, Roy.   "Old Christmas Morning"
"Lonesome Water"   (Kentucky Mountains)

Lanier, Sidney.   "That's More in the Man Than Thar Is in the Land"
and others   (Middle Georgia)

Lowell, James Russell.   *Biglow Papers*   (Boston Yankee)

Riley, James Whitcomb.   "When the Frost Is on the Punkin'"
"Wortermelon Time"
"The Little Town of Tailholt"
"The Ole Swimmin' Hole"   (Indiana)

SHORT STORIES

Benét, Stephen Vincent.   *Thirteen O'clock*   (Georgia)

Cable, George Washington.   *Old Creole Days*   (New Orleans)

Cather, Willa.   *Obscure Destinies*   (Nebraska)

Dunne, Finley Peter.   *Mr. Dooley in Peace and War*
Mr. Dooley's Philosophy
Mr. Dooley Says
Mr. Dooley on Making a Will
    and others   (Chicago Irish)

Freeman, Mary Wilkins.   *A Humble Romance and Other Stories*
A New England Nun and Other Stories
People of Our Neighborhood   (New England)

Garland, Hamlin.   "Under the Lion's Paw"   (Midwest)

Harris, George Washington.   *Sut Lovingood Yarns*   (Tennessee)

Harris, Joel Chandler.   *Uncle Remus: His Songs and His Sayings*
Nights with Uncle Remus
Mingo and Other Sketches in Black and White
Free Joe and Other Georgian Sketches
    (Middle Georgia)

Jewett, Sarah Orne.   *Country of the Pointed Firs and Other Stories*
    (New England)

Kober, Arthur.   *Oooh, What You Said!*
Pardon Me for Pointing
My Dear Bella
That Man Is Here Again
Bella, Bella Kissed a Fella   (New York City Yiddish)

Murfree, Mary Noailles   ("Charles Egbert Craddock").
In the Tennessee Mountains   (East Tennessee)

Page, Thomas Nelson.   *In Ole Virginia*   (Negro of the Virginia Plantation)

Runyon, Damon.   *More Guys and Dolls*   (New York City)

Singmaster, Elsie.   "The Belsnickel"   (Pennsylvania Dutch)

Stuart, Jesse.   "Uncle Jeff,"   *Head o' W-Hollow*
"Another April,"   *Tales from the Plum Grove Hills*
    (Kentucky)

[Note: *American Book Collector*, September 1958 issue, is devoted to Jesse Stuart and contains full bibliographical data for 260 short stories by Stuart.]

Townsend, Edward.   *"Chimmie Fadden," Major Max, and Other Stories*
Chimmie Fadden Explains, Major Max Expounds   (New York City)

Twain, Mark.   "The Celebrated Jumping Frog of Calaveras County"
"Baker's Blue-Jay Yarn"   (Far West)

West, Jessamyn.   "The Battle of Finney's Ford"   (Quakers)

NOVELS

Cable, George Washington.   *The Grandissimes*
Madame Delphine   (New Orleans)

Cather, Willa.   *O Pioneers!*
My Antonia   (Nebraska)

Eggleston, Edward.   *The Circuit Rider*   (Southern Indiana)

Haun, Mildred.   *That Hawk's Done Gone*   (East Tennessee)

Murfree, Mary Noailles   ("Charles Egbert Craddock").
The Prophet of the Great Smoky Mountains
(East Tennessee)

Page, Thomas Nelson.   *Red Rock*   (Negro of the Virginia Plantation)

Perry, George Sessions.   *Hold Autumn in Your Hand*   (Texas)

Rawlings, Majorie Kinnan.   *The Yearling*   (Northern Florida)

Simms, William Gilmore.   *Guy Rivers*
Richard Hurdis
The Border Beagles   (Old Southwest Frontier)
The Partisan
Mellichamp
Katharine Walton
Woodcraft
The Forayers   (South Carolina)

Smith, Seba.   *My Thirty Years Out of the Senate*
Life and Writings of Jack Downing   (Maine)

Twain, Mark.   *Roughing It*   (Far West)
Huckleberry Finn   (Mississippi River)

PLAYS

Bradford, Roark.   *John Henry*   (Louisiana, Mississippi)

Greene, Patterson.   *Papa Is All*   (Pennsylvania Dutch Region)

Kober, Arthur.   *Having Wonderful Time*   (New York City Yiddish)

Van Druten, John.   *I Remember Mama*   (San Francisco Norwegian)

SUGGESTIONS FOR STUDY

Analyze Dialect in Literature

Using one of the selections assigned for class work or one chosen for a report, compile the following three lists to file for reference in your notebook: (1) devices used to indicate differences in pronunciation (try to avoid "eye dialect"); (2) words showing differences in vocabulary; and (3) those indicating differences in grammar.

Test Your Comprehension

1. For what specific purposes may authors use dialect?

2. Why does the approximation of dialect in writing present problems to the writer?

3. Name several American authors who have made use of dialect in their works.

4. Define and illustrate the term "eye dialect."

5. What difficulties in writing dialect are brought about by the regional character of dialect in the United States?

Add to Your Vocabulary

Select from this text five words that you would like to master for your own use. After verifying their meanings by using the dictionary, use each one in a sentence of your own.

Report on the Use of Dialect in Literature

Select a poem, short story, or novel for a report on the use of regional American dialect in written English. You may make a choice from the list of selections furnished in this text or from the shelves of your library. In the latter instance, be sure that the dialect used is genuine and not merely assumed for the sake of achieving a certain effect such as quaintness or humor. In your analysis of written dialect, consider the following points: What purpose does the use of dialect serve in the piece of literature studied? Does it entertain, develop or add to the setting, supply local color, sharpen the impression made by a character, or define a mood? What devices does the author use to indicate differences in pronunciation? Give examples of various kinds of word changes. List words showing vocabulary differences, and define their meanings as they occur in context. What differences in grammar do you find? List and discuss the most commonly used as well as the most unusual examples of these. Is the author consistent in the use of dialect? Would it be possible for anyone not already familiar with this dialect to realize its effect from the written representation?

Listen to Records

With recorded as with written dialect, a distinction should be made between the genuine and the spurious. Ballad records employ both kinds. One example of genuine dialect occurs in the Leadbelly records which demonstrate the speech typical of the uneducated Southern Negro (Folkways Records).

INDEX